## Beef up your revision muscles with CGP!

It's not easy to rack up a high score in GCSE PE — and the latest Grade 9-1 course is tougher than ever. Luckily, help is at hand...

This brilliant CGP Revision Guide explains everything you need to know for the Edexcel exams, from dorsi-flexion to data analysis! There are also plenty of exam-style questions to test you on what you've learned.

We've also included advice on how to pick up as many marks as possible, so you'll be ready to tackle your exams and finish with style.

## CGP — still the best! ☺

Our sole aim here at CGP is to produce the highest quality books — carefully written, immaculately presented and dangerously close to being funny.

Then we work our socks off to get them out to you
— at the cheapest possible prices.

# Contents

## Section One — Anatomy and Physiology

The Skeletal System...................................................................................1
The Muscular System..................................................................................4
The Cardiovascular System.........................................................................6
The Respiratory System..............................................................................8
Aerobic and Anaerobic Exercise................................................................10
Short-Term Effects of Exercise..................................................................11
Long-Term Effects of Exercise...................................................................13
Revision Questions for Section One..........................................................14

## Section Two — Movement Analysis

Lever Systems............................................................................................15
Planes and Axes of Movement...................................................................16
Revision Questions for Section Two..........................................................17

## Section Three — Physical Training

Health and Fitness......................................................................................18
Components of Fitness...............................................................................19
Fitness Testing...........................................................................................23
Principles of Training.................................................................................25
Training Target Zones................................................................................27
Training Methods.......................................................................................28
Preventing Injuries.....................................................................................31
Injuries and Treatment...............................................................................32
Performance-Enhancing Drugs..................................................................34
Revision Questions for Section Three.......................................................35

*Component 1 — Fitness and Body Systems*

## Section Four — Health, Fitness and Well-being

Health, Fitness and Well-being ........................................................................ 36
Lifestyle Choices ............................................................................................. 38
Sedentary Lifestyle .......................................................................................... 39
Diet and Nutrition ........................................................................................... 40
Diet, Nutrition and Performance ...................................................................... 42
Optimum Weight ............................................................................................. 43
Revision Questions for Section Four ................................................................ 44

## Section Five — Sport Psychology

Skills and Practice ........................................................................................... 45
Goal Setting .................................................................................................... 46
Guidance and Feedback .................................................................................. 47
Revision Questions for Section Five ................................................................. 48

## Section Six — Sport, Society and Culture

Influences on Participation .............................................................................. 49
Commercialisation of Sport ............................................................................. 51
Sporting Behaviour .......................................................................................... 53
Revision Questions for Section Six .................................................................. 54

## Section Seven — Using Data (for Components 1 & 2)

Using Data ...................................................................................................... 55

Answering Exam Questions ............................................................................. 58

Answers .......................................................................................................... 60
Glossary .......................................................................................................... 64
Index ............................................................................................................... 67

*Component 2 — Health and Performance*

Published by CGP

Editors:
Chris Corrall, Joanna Daniels and Alison Palin.

Contributor:
Paddy Gannon

With thanks to Chris Cope and Glenn Rogers for the proofreading.

With thanks to Ana Pungartnik for the copyright research.

Definitions from Edexcel specifications used with the permission of Pearson Education.

Definition of health on page 18 is from the preamble to the Constitution of the World Health Organization, as adopted by the International Health Conference, New York, 19 June - 22 July 1946; signed on 22 July 1946 by the representatives of 61 States (Official Records of the World Health Organization, no. 2, p.100), and entered into force on 7 April 1948.

Normative data table for grip dynamometer test on page 24 was published in 'Physical Education and the Study of Sport' 4th ed, 2002, Davis ed, p.123, 1 table ('Normative data table for grip strength test' for 16 to 19 year olds), Copyright Elsevier (2016).

Normative data for 35 m sprint test on page 24 from ARKINSTALL, M et al. (2010) VCE Physical Education 2. Malaysia: Macmillan. p.250. © Reproduced by permission of Macmillan Education Australia.

Data about obesity rates on page 39 copyright © 2015, Health and Social Care Information Centre. All rights reserved.

Graph of participation rates in sports on page 50 based on data from Sport England.

Source for data about shirt sponsorship in the Premier League on page 52: sportingintelligence.com.

ISBN: 978 1 78294 533 8
Printed by Elanders Ltd, Newcastle upon Tyne.
Clipart from Corel®

Text, design, layout and original illustrations © Coordination Group Publications Ltd (CGP) 2016
All rights reserved.

Based on the classic CGP style created by Richard Parsons.

Photocopying more than one section of this book is not permitted, even if you have a CLA licence.
Extra copies are available from CGP with next day delivery • 0800 1712 712 • www.cgpbooks.co.uk

# Section One — Anatomy and Physiology

# The Skeletal System

Welcome to the GCSE PE fun bus — first stop is the skeleton. It gives the body its shape and has loads of jobs to do. It's made up of various kinds of bones, all with their own function. Here we go...

## The Skeleton has Different Functions

The skeleton does more than you might think to help your performance in sport. Its main functions are:

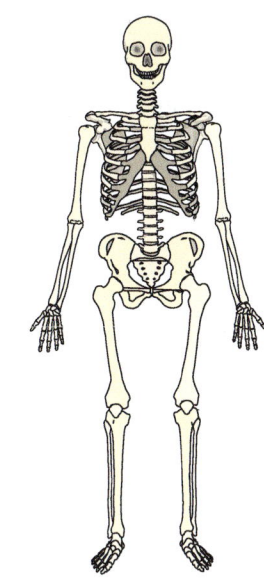

**① SUPPORT/SHAPE:**
1) The skeleton is a rigid bone frame for the rest of the body. Our shape is mainly due to our skeleton.
2) The skeleton supports the soft tissues like skin and muscle.
3) This helps you to have good posture, which is essential in loads of sports.
4) E.g. good posture aids performance in gymnastics.

**③ MOVEMENT:**
1) Muscles, attached to bones by tendons, can move bones at joints.
2) This movement is essential for good performance in sport.
3) There are different types of movement at the various joints, which are important in different sports.

**② PROTECTION:**
1) Bones are very tough — they protect vital organs like the brain, heart and lungs.
2) This allows you to perform well in sport without fear of serious injury.
3) E.g. the skull protects the brain, so you can head a football or take punches in a boxing match without serious injury.

**④ MAKING BLOOD CELLS/PLATELETS:**
1) Some bones contain bone marrow, which makes the components of blood — platelets and red and white blood cells (see p7).
2) Red blood cells are really important during exercise — they transport the oxygen that muscles need to move.
3) Athletes with more red blood cells perform better — more oxygen can be delivered to their muscles.

**⑤ MINERAL STORAGE:**
1) Bones store minerals like calcium and phosphorus.
2) These help with bone strength — so you're less likely to break a bone.
3) They're also needed for muscle contraction — so the body can move.

## There are Different Types of Bone in the Skeleton

There are four main types of bone in the skeleton. Each type is suited to a different purpose.

**Long Bones**
Long bones (e.g. the humerus in the arm) are strong and are used by muscles to assist movement.

**Short Bones**
Short bones (e.g. the tarsals in the foot) support the weight of the body — they're weight-bearing.

*Short bones are also used in some smaller body movements, e.g. moving the hand at the wrist.*

**Irregular Bones**
Irregular bones (e.g. the vertebrae of the spine) are suited to protection and muscle attachment.

**Flat Bones**
Flat bones (e.g. the ribs) protect internal organs. Their broad surface also allows muscle attachment.

Have no fear — I'll protect you.

Aw, thanks.

## I bet you found that all extremely humerus...

It's really important that you remember the different types of bone in the skeleton — but make sure you learn what they all do, too, and their roles in helping you play sport. In the meantime, give this Exam Practice Question a go.

Q1 Explain how long bones aid performance in physical activity and sport. [2 marks]

# The Skeletal System

Time for some more skeleton-related fun — this page'll give you a hand at remembering the names of some important bones in the body, their types and what they do. I bet you can hardly wait...

## Learn the Structure of the Skeleton

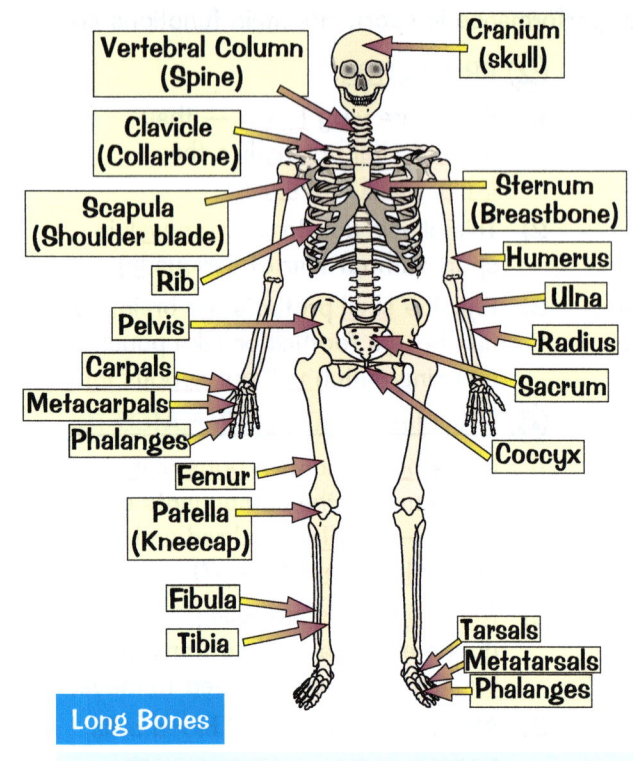

Skeleton diagram labels:
- Vertebral Column (Spine)
- Cranium (skull)
- Clavicle (Collarbone)
- Scapula (Shoulder blade)
- Sternum (Breastbone)
- Humerus
- Rib
- Ulna
- Pelvis
- Radius
- Carpals
- Sacrum
- Metacarpals
- Coccyx
- Phalanges
- Femur
- Patella (Kneecap)
- Fibula
- Tibia
- Tarsals
- Metatarsals
- Phalanges

### Flat Bones

Cranium — protects the brain.
Sternum and ribs — protect the heart and lungs. The ribs also protect the kidneys.
Scapula — has many muscles attached to it, helping arm and shoulder movement.
Pelvis — has many muscles attached to it, helping leg movement.

### Short Bones

Carpals — form the wrist and give it stability, allowing movement of the hand.
Tarsals — bear the body's weight when on foot, e.g. during standing and running.

The patella is a different type of bone — it's a sesamoid bone. It protects the tendon that crosses the knee joint by stopping it rubbing against the femur.

### Long Bones

Clavicle — forms part of the shoulder joint to assist arm movement.
Humerus — used by muscles to move the whole arm, e.g. swinging a badminton racket.
Ulna and radius — used by muscles to move the lower arm, e.g. bending at the elbow.
Femur — used by muscles to move the whole leg, e.g. when running.
Fibula and tibia — used by muscles to move the lower leg, e.g. to kick a football.
Metacarpals — used by muscles to allow the hand to grip, e.g. to hold a cricket ball.
Phalanges — used by muscles to move and bend the fingers and toes.
Metatarsals — used by muscles to move the foot, e.g. when jumping.

## Learn the Structure of the Vertebral Column

The vertebral column ('spine' or 'spinal column') is made up of irregular bones called vertebrae. It can be divided into five regions:

Cervical — Seven vertebrae at the top of the spine.
Thoracic — Twelve vertebrae below the cervical region.
Lumbar — Five vertebrae below the thoracic region.
Sacrum — Five vertebrae fused together below the lumbar region.
Coccyx — Four vertebrae fused together at the bottom of the spine.

The vertebral column protects the spinal cord.

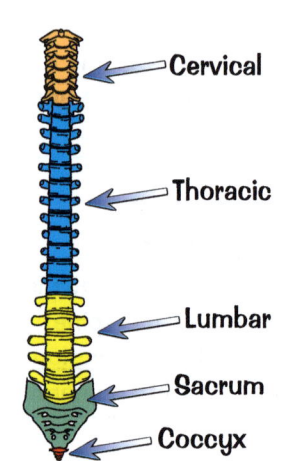

Vertebral column diagram labels: Cervical, Thoracic, Lumbar, Sacrum, Coccyx

### Now, use your phalanges to pick up a pen and paper...

Now you know all about the skeleton's structure, give this Exam Practice Question a go.

Q1  Which one of the following is a long bone located in the hand?
    A  Carpal    B  Tarsal    C  Metacarpal    D  Radius          [1 mark]

# The Skeletal System

You'll need to know about some other important bits in the skeleton — joints (and the ways they can move) and connective tissues. Luckily, all the info you need is right here on this page. Amazing...

## There are Different Kinds of Joint Movement

Joints are any points where two or more bones meet.
There are eight joint movements that you need to know:

*See page 16 for more on movement.*

**FLEXION** 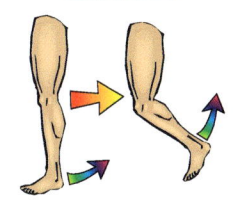
Closing a joint, e.g. the wrist movement during a basketball throw.

**EXTENSION** 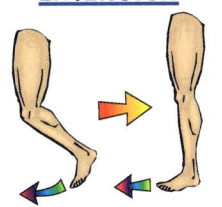
Opening a joint, e.g. kicking a football.

**ADDUCTION** 
Moving towards an imaginary centre line, e.g. swinging a golf club.

**ABDUCTION** 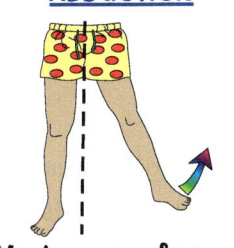
Moving away from an imaginary centre line, e.g. bringing back a tennis racket before swinging it.

**ROTATION** 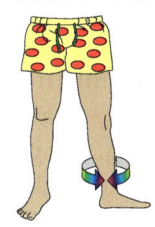
Clockwise or anticlockwise movement, e.g. the leg movement during a turnout in ballet.

**CIRCUMDUCTION** 
Movement of a limb, hand or foot in a circular motion, e.g. to bowl a cricket ball.

**PLANTAR-FLEXION** 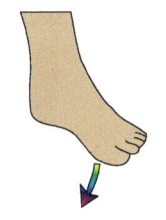
Extension at the ankle, e.g. pointing the toes during gymnastics.

**DORSI-FLEXION** 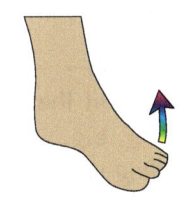
Flexion at the ankle, e.g. lifting the toes during gymnastics.

## There are Four Joint Types You Need to Know

You need to know about ball and socket, pivot, hinge and condyloid joints. Each type allows a certain range of movements.

| type | examples | flexion and extension | adduction and abduction | rotation | circumduction |
|---|---|---|---|---|---|
| ball and socket | hip, shoulder | ✓ | ✓ | ✓ | ✓ |
| hinge | knee, ankle, elbow | ✓ | ✗ | ✗ | ✗ |
| condyloid | wrist | ✓ | ✓ | ✗ | ✓ |
| pivot | neck (atlas and axis) | ✗ | ✗ | ✓ | ✗ |

*The atlas and axis are the top two vertebrae of the spine.*

## Connective Tissues Join Muscle and Bones

There are three types of connective tissue you need to know about.

**CARTILAGE** — acts as a cushion between bones to prevent damage during joint movement.

**LIGAMENTS** — hold bones together to help maintain the stability of the skeleton during movement. They're made of tough and fibrous tissue (like very strong string).

**TENDONS** — attach muscles to bones (or to other muscles) to allow bones to move when muscles contract.

Section One — Anatomy and Physiology

# The Muscular System

The skeletal system can't make the body move on its own — it needs some help from the muscular system. Together, they're known as the musculo-skeletal system.

## There are Two Different Types of Muscle

1) Like the title says, there are two different types of muscle you need to know. These are...

   **VOLUNTARY MUSCLES**
   Attached to the skeleton and are under your control. They help to move the body.

   **INVOLUNTARY MUSCLES**
   Work internal organs without effort from you, e.g. muscles in blood vessels control the amount of blood flowing to voluntary muscles.

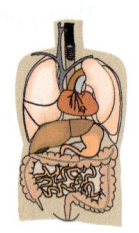

2) Cardiac muscle is a type of involuntary muscle that forms the heart.
3) It never gets tired — the heart can pump blood around your body all the time.
4) During exercise, voluntary muscles need oxygen so they can move the body. When the heart beats, it pumps blood carrying oxygen to these muscles.

## Each Muscle has a Specific Function

You need to learn the names of some voluntary muscles, and what their main functions are.

**BICEPS** — flexion at the elbow, e.g. when curling weights.

**TRICEPS** — extension at the elbow, e.g. during a jump shot in netball.

**PECTORALIS MAJOR** — adduction and flexion (horizontally) at the shoulder, e.g. during a forehand drive in tennis.

**HIP FLEXORS** — flexion of the leg at the hip, e.g. lifting the knee when sprinting.

**GLUTEUS MAXIMUS** — extension of the leg at the hip, e.g. pushing the body forward when running.

**DELTOID** — flexion, extension, abduction or circumduction at the shoulder. E.g. during front crawl in swimming.

**LATISSIMUS DORSI** — extension, adduction or rotation at the shoulder, e.g. during butterfly stroke in swimming.

**HAMSTRINGS** — flexion at the knee, e.g. bringing the foot back before kicking a football.

**QUADRICEPS** — extension at the knee, e.g. when performing a drop kick in rugby.

**GASTROCNEMIUS** — plantar-flexion at the ankle, e.g. standing on the toes in ballet pointe work.

**TIBIALIS ANTERIOR** — dorsi-flexion at the ankle, e.g. during a heel side turn in snowboarding.

**EXTERNAL OBLIQUES** — rotation or flexion at the waist, e.g. preparing to throw a discus.

Muscles labelled on diagram: pectoralis major, deltoids, biceps, external obliques, hip flexors, quadriceps, tibialis anterior, triceps, latissimus dorsi, gluteus maximus, hamstrings, gastrocnemius (calf).

### My muscles don't feel like they volunteer for anything...

Make sure you can name all these muscles and describe their functions — including examples of when they're used in specific sports. Oh, and don't forget to try this Practice Question.

Q1 State the muscle group that works to produce the hip movement when bringing the leg forward to kick a football. [1 mark]

Section One — Anatomy and Physiology

# The Muscular System

Now on to more stuff about muscles — just what we were all hoping for. This page'll cover how muscles actually make all those fancy movements happen, and what they're made of, too.

## Antagonistic Muscles Work in Pairs

Muscles can only do one thing — pull. To make a joint move in two directions, you need two muscles that can pull in opposite directions.

1) Antagonistic muscles are pairs of muscles that work against each other.
2) One muscle contracts while the other one relaxes, and vice versa.
3) The muscle that's contracting to produce the movement is the agonist.
4) The muscle that's relaxing is the antagonist.
5) Each muscle is attached to two bones by tendons.
6) Only one of the bones connected at the joint actually moves.

*Here, 'contracts' means 'shortens', and 'relaxes' means 'lengthens'. But you might see 'contracts' used to mean 'creates tension' — which muscles do when they shorten and lengthen.*

There are antagonistic muscle pairs at different joints in the body:

**KNEE — hamstrings & quadriceps**

Flexion — agonist — hamstrings
antagonist — quadriceps

Extension — agonist — quadriceps
antagonist — hamstrings

**ELBOW — biceps & triceps**

Flexion — agonist — biceps
antagonist — triceps

Extension — agonist — triceps
antagonist — biceps

**HIP — hip flexors & gluteus maximus**

Flexion — agonist — hip flexors
antagonist — gluteus maximus

Extension — agonist — gluteus maximus
antagonist — hip flexors

**ANKLE — gastrocnemius & tibialis anterior**

Plantar-flexion — agonist — gastrocnemius
antagonist — tibialis anterior

Dorsi-flexion — agonist — tibialis anterior
antagonist — gastrocnemius

## Different Types of Muscle Fibre suit Different Activities

1) All muscles are made up of fibres.
2) These muscle fibres can be slow twitch (type I) or fast twitch (type IIA and type IIX).

**SLOW TWITCH**

TYPE I — Suited to low intensity aerobic work (e.g. marathon running) as they can be used for a long period of time without fatiguing.

*See p10 for the definitions of aerobic and anaerobic work.*

**FAST TWITCH**

TYPE IIA — Used in anaerobic work, but can be improved through endurance training to increase their resistance to fatigue.

TYPE IIX — Used in anaerobic work. Can generate a much greater force than other fibre types but fatigue quickly. Useful in short bursts of exercise, e.g. a 100 m sprint.

---

### Is that a bacon rope I see? Nope, it's a hamstring...

So, type I fibres are good for long periods of exercise, but in a sprint they'd probably just get you last place. Types IIA and IIX are good for short bursts, but not for long slogs. With that in mind, have a go at this Practice Question.

Q1 Which one of the following muscle fibre types is best suited for use in a long distance triathlon?

    **A** Type I     **B** Type IIA     **C** Type IIX     **D** Fast twitch          [1 mark]

*Section One — Anatomy and Physiology*

# The Cardiovascular System

Your cardiovascular system's job is to move blood around your body. As the blood travels around, it does loads of really useful stuff to help you take part in physical activity and sport. Read on to find out more...

## The Cardiovascular System has Three Main Functions

**TRANSPORT OF SUBSTANCES** — Transporting things around the body in the bloodstream, like oxygen, carbon dioxide, and nutrients (e.g. glucose). This gives the muscles what they need to release energy to move during exercise (and takes away any waste products).

*Have a look at p10 for more about how muscles use oxygen and glucose.*

**TEMPERATURE CONTROL** — Moving more blood nearer the skin cools the body more quickly. This means you can exercise for a long time without overheating.

**CLOTTING OF WOUNDS** — Your blood clots to seal cuts. This stops you bleeding too much if you get a cut, and helps to prevent wounds becoming infected.

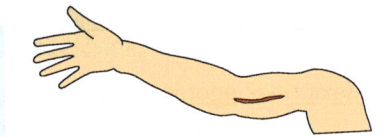

## Learn How the Heart Pumps Blood Around the Body

1) The cardiovascular system is made up of three main parts — the heart, blood and blood vessels.

   *Arteries, veins and capillaries are the main types of blood vessel.*

2) During any kind of physical activity, blood needs to circulate around the body to deliver oxygen and glucose to your muscles, and to take carbon dioxide away from them. This is where the heart comes in:

**LEFT SIDE**
- Oxygenated blood from the lungs enters the left atrium through the pulmonary veins.
- The left atrium contracts, pushing the blood through the bicuspid valve into the left ventricle.
- The left ventricle contracts, pushing the blood through the left semi-lunar valve into the aorta (an artery), which carries the oxygenated blood to the rest of the body — including the muscles.

**RIGHT SIDE**
- When the muscles have used the oxygen in the blood, it becomes deoxygenated.
- It then enters the right atrium through the vena cava vein.
- The right atrium contracts, pushing the blood through the tricuspid valve into the right ventricle.
- The right ventricle contracts, pushing the blood through the right semi-lunar valve into the pulmonary artery, which carries the blood to the lungs to be oxygenated again.

*The 'left's and 'right's on the diagram refer to the person whose heart it is — that's why they're reversed.*

### The heart — it's all just pump and circumstance...

To sum up, the heart is pretty important. It makes sure that the blood gets oxygenated, then gets it to where it needs to be to deliver that oxygen. Now, get learning that heart diagram, and try this Practice Question.

Q1  Analyse the role of the pulmonary artery in physical activity and sport.  [4 marks]

Section One — Anatomy and Physiology

# The Cardiovascular System

When you start to exercise, your muscles have to nick some blood from other parts of the body. Charming...

## Arteries, Veins and Capillaries Carry Blood

1) Blood vessels transport blood — they have a hollow centre called the lumen so blood can flow through.
2) Different types of blood vessel are suited to different roles:

**ARTERIES** — carry blood away from the heart. All arteries carry oxygenated blood except for the pulmonary arteries. Their thick, muscular walls allow them to carry blood flowing at high pressure.

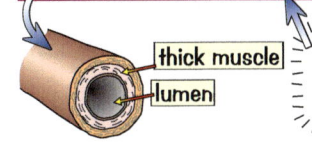

**VEINS** — carry blood towards the heart. All veins carry deoxygenated blood, except for the pulmonary veins. They carry blood at low pressure, so they have thinner walls and less muscle than arteries.

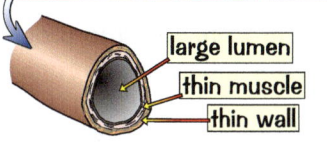

**CAPILLARIES** — carry blood through the body to exchange oxygen, carbon dioxide and nutrients with the body's tissues. They have very thin walls so substances can easily pass through.

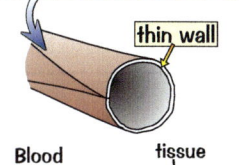

*Blood pressure is how strongly the blood presses against the walls of blood vessels.*

3) There are also two other small types of blood vessel — arterioles (which branch off arteries) and venules (which meet to form veins).
4) Oxygenated blood flows through arteries into arterioles, then into capillaries.
5) After gases have been exchanged between the capillaries and the body tissues, blood is transported from the capillaries into venules, where it flows back into the veins.

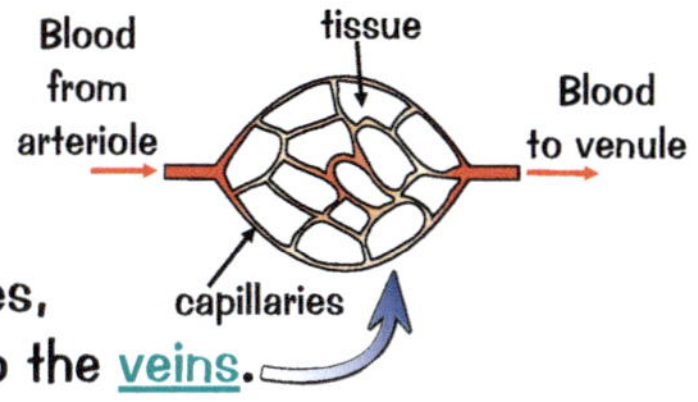

## Your Blood Vessels Change when you Exercise

When you exercise, blood is redistributed around the body to increase the supply of oxygen to your muscles — this is known as 'vascular shunting'.

① When you exercise, your arteries widen to stop your blood pressure getting too high...

② ...and to make the most of your blood supply, blood that would usually go to organs like the gut and liver is shunted to the muscles...

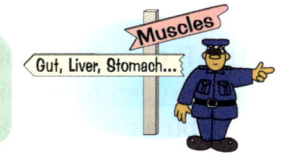

③ ...by blood vessels in the muscles widening (vasodilation) to let in more blood...

④ ...or blood vessels in the inactive organs narrowing (vasoconstriction) to restrict the amount of blood that can flow in.

*Think about which body parts will or won't be active during different activities. Some organs (e.g. the brain) need to stay active during exercise.*

Ⓐ Also, as your muscles work, they generate heat — which warms your blood...

Ⓑ ...and this blood is shunted closer to your skin, so the heat can escape through radiation.

*Which makes you go red.*

Ⓒ And you also start to sweat, which helps keep you cool.

## Your Blood is made up of Cells, Platelets and Plasma

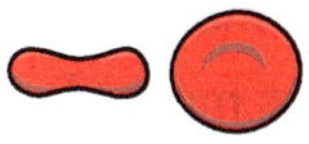

**RED BLOOD CELLS** — Carry oxygen around the body so it can be used to release energy needed by muscles during physical activity.

**WHITE BLOOD CELLS** — Fight against disease so you stay healthy and perform well (see p18).

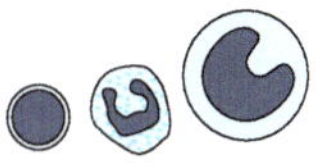

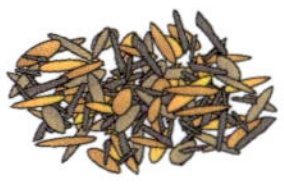

**PLATELETS** — Help blood to clot at wounds so they don't become infected.

**PLASMA** — carries everything in the bloodstream. That includes blood cells, digested food (e.g. glucose) and waste (e.g. carbon dioxide).

---

## Romantic comedies — exercise for your heart...

Remember, vascular shunting happens during exercise because your muscles need blood more than some of your organs do. And this couldn't happen without vasodilation and vasoconstriction. Now on to a Practice Question...

Q1 Analyse the role of plasma during participation in physical activity and sport. [4 marks]

Section One — Anatomy and Physiology

# The Respiratory System

You'll probably recognise most of this stuff from biology — but there's no harm in a quick recap.

## Learn the Structure of the Respiratory System

The respiratory system is everything you use to breathe.
It's found in the chest cavity — the area inside the chest.

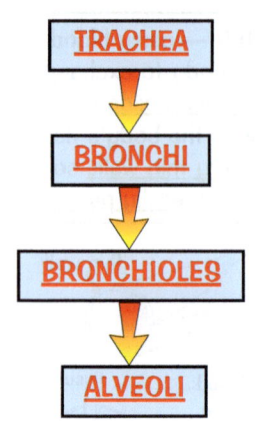

**TRACHEA → BRONCHI → BRONCHIOLES → ALVEOLI**

1) Air passes through the nose or mouth and then on to the trachea.
2) The trachea splits into two tubes called bronchi (each one is a 'bronchus') — one going to each lung.
3) The bronchi split into progressively smaller tubes called bronchioles.
4) The bronchioles finally end at small bags called alveoli (each one is an 'alveolus') where gases are exchanged (see below).

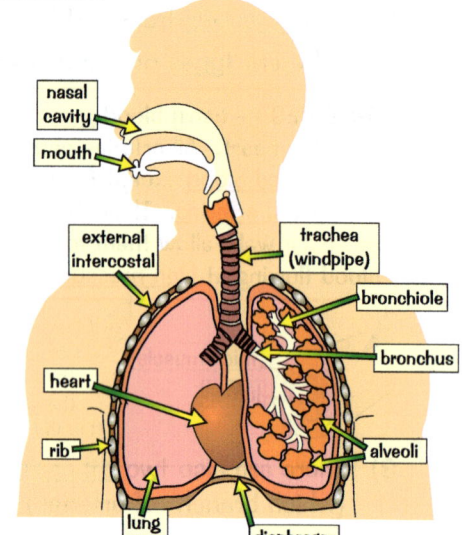

The diaphragm and external intercostal muscles help the air to move in and out:

- When you breathe in, the diaphragm and external intercostals contract to move the ribcage upwards and expand the chest cavity. This draws air into your lungs.
- When you breathe out, the diaphragm and the external intercostals relax, moving the ribcage down and shrinking the chest cavity. This forces air back out of the lungs the same way it came in.

## Oxygen and Carbon Dioxide are Exchanged in the Alveoli

1) The cardiovascular and respiratory systems have to work together to get oxygen to the muscles, and carbon dioxide away from them. They do this by exchanging gases between the alveoli and capillaries surrounding them.

*The cardiovascular and respiratory systems together make up the cardio-respiratory system.*

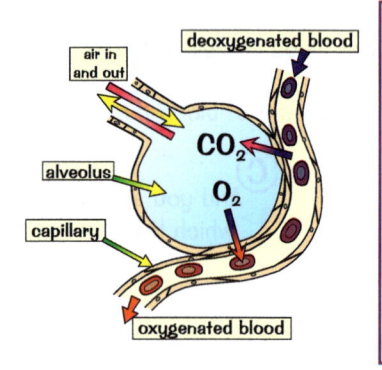

1) Oxygenated blood delivers oxygen and collects carbon dioxide as it circulates around the body. Deoxygenated blood returns to the heart and is then pumped to the lungs.
2) In the lungs, carbon dioxide moves from the blood in the capillaries into the alveoli so it can be breathed out.
3) Oxygen from the air you breathe into the lungs moves across from the alveoli to the red blood cells in the capillaries.
4) The oxygenated blood returns to the heart and is pumped to the rest of the body. The red blood cells carry the oxygen around the body and deliver it where it's needed, e.g. the muscles.

2) Alveoli have a large surface area and very thin walls — so gases can easily pass through them.
3) This exchange of gases happens through a process called diffusion. This means the gases move down a concentration gradient — from a place of higher concentration to a place of lower concentration:

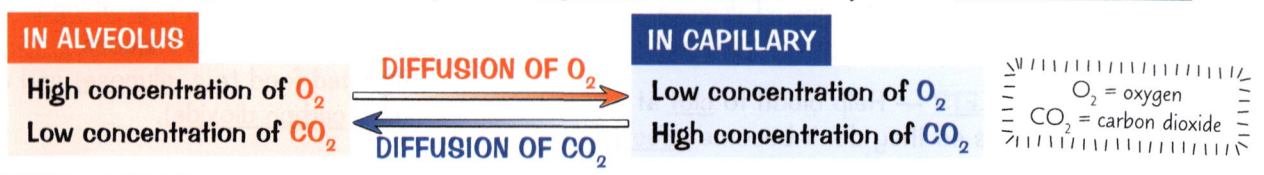

| IN ALVEOLUS | | IN CAPILLARY |
|---|---|---|
| High concentration of $O_2$ | DIFFUSION OF $O_2$ → | Low concentration of $O_2$ |
| Low concentration of $CO_2$ | ← DIFFUSION OF $CO_2$ | High concentration of $CO_2$ |

$O_2$ = oxygen
$CO_2$ = carbon dioxide

### Air we go — keeping trachea respiratory system...

So, diffusion helps the cardiovascular and respiratory systems work together to exchange oxygen and carbon dioxide. Pretty impressive, eh? I bet you'll be impressed with this Exam Practice Question, too.

Q1 Explain how deoxygenated blood becomes oxygenated. [3 marks]

Section One — Anatomy and Physiology

# The Respiratory System

You might have noticed that you take bigger breaths when you exercise. That's just 'cos the air we breathe in contains the stuff we need more of for exercise, and the air we breathe out contains the stuff we don't want.

## Air is made up of Different Gases

1) You need to know the composition of the air we inhale (breathe in) and exhale (breathe out). This just means the different gases it's made up of.

|  | % of inhaled air | % of exhaled air |
|---|---|---|
| Oxygen | 21% | 16% |
| Carbon dioxide | 0.04% | 4% |
| Nitrogen (as well as argon and other gases) | 79% | 79% |

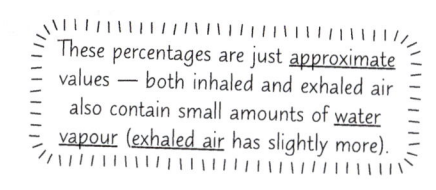

*These percentages are just approximate values — both inhaled and exhaled air also contain small amounts of water vapour (exhaled air has slightly more).*

2) Exhaled air contains less oxygen than inhaled air. This is because some of the oxygen in inhaled air is used up by the body to release energy through aerobic respiration.

3) Exhaled air also contains more carbon dioxide than inhaled air. This is because carbon dioxide is produced when energy is released through aerobic respiration. The body needs to get rid of this carbon dioxide, so we breathe it out.

## Tidal Volume Increases during Exercise

1) The amount of air you breathe in or out during one breath is known as your tidal volume.
2) During exercise, your tidal volume increases — you breathe more deeply. This happens for a couple of reasons:

- To bring in more oxygen. This helps to release extra energy in the muscles (during aerobic activity) and remove lactic acid from them (produced during anaerobic activity).
- To breathe out the extra carbon dioxide produced during aerobic activity.

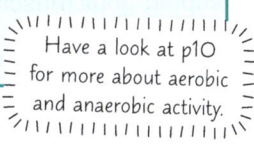

*Have a look at p10 for more about aerobic and anaerobic activity.*

## Vital Capacity — the Most Air you can Breathe In

1) Your tidal volume is only a fraction of your vital capacity:

> **VITAL CAPACITY** — the most air you could possibly breathe in after breathing out the largest volume of air you can.

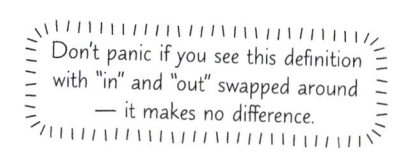

*Don't panic if you see this definition with "in" and "out" swapped around — it makes no difference.*

2) The larger your vital capacity, the more oxygen you can take in and absorb into your bloodstream in each breath — and the more oxygen you can supply to your muscles.
3) You can increase your vital capacity through exercise — see page 13.

---

### Breathe iiiiiiiiiiiiiiiiiin — and oooooooouuuuuut...

Make sure you revise the compositions of inhaled and exhaled air until you can remember them without looking at this page. Keep scribbling them down until you can't forget them. And give this Practice Question a go.

Q1   Explain why an athlete would benefit from a high vital capacity.   [3 marks]

Section One — Anatomy and Physiology

# Aerobic and Anaerobic Exercise

Your body can release energy using two types of respiration — it all depends on how hard you're exercising. And different sources of fuel can be used during respiration. Fantastic stuff.

## Aerobic Respiration — With Oxygen

1) All the living cells in your body need energy. Normally the body uses oxygen to release energy from glucose (a sugar found in food). This is called aerobic respiration.

> Glucose + Oxygen → Carbon dioxide + Water + Energy

*Carbon dioxide and water are by-products of aerobic respiration.*

2) If your body's keeping up with the oxygen demand of its cells, it means there's enough oxygen available for aerobic respiration.

3) Activities where your body can keep up with oxygen demand are called aerobic activities.

> **AEROBIC ACTIVITY:** 'with oxygen'. If the exercise you're doing isn't too fast and you're exercising at a steady rate, your heart and lungs can supply your muscles with all the oxygen they need.

4) You breathe out the carbon dioxide through your lungs, while the water is lost as sweat, urine, or in the air you breathe out.

5) As long as your muscles are supplied with enough oxygen, you can do aerobic exercise — so if you're exercising for long periods, you'll be producing your energy aerobically.

6) Aerobic respiration is how marathon runners get their energy.

## Anaerobic Respiration — Without Oxygen

1) During vigorous exercise, your body can't supply all the oxygen needed. When this happens, your muscles release energy without using oxygen in a different process called anaerobic respiration.

> Glucose → Lactic acid + Energy

*Lactic acid is a by-product of anaerobic respiration.*

2) Activities where your body has to do this are called anaerobic activities.

> **ANAEROBIC ACTIVITY:** 'without oxygen'. If you exercise in short, intense bursts, your heart and lungs can't supply your muscles with oxygen as fast as your cells use it.

3) The lack of oxygen during anaerobic respiration means it can only provide energy for short periods of time — so you can't exercise at high intensity for very long.

4) Anaerobic respiration is how sprinters get their energy.

## Carbohydrates and Fats are used as Fuel

1) Your body needs a source of fuel so that respiration can provide energy.
2) Carbohydrates (from foods such as pasta) and fats stored in the body can both be used as fuel.

> **CARBOHYDRATES** — the body's main source of fuel. They're used during aerobic activities at moderate intensity and for high intensity anaerobic activities.

> **FATS** — used as fuel for aerobic activity at low intensity. Fats provide more energy than carbohydrates, but they can't be used as fuel for higher intensity activities.

---

### Have you met Anna Robic? She's an excellent sprinter...

Aerobic respiration is much more efficient, so the body uses it whenever it can. Make sure you know the difference between aerobic and anaerobic activity, and the fuels used for them. Try this Practice Question, too.

Q1  Explain why a 100 metre sprint would be an anaerobic activity.        [3 marks]

*Section One — Anatomy and Physiology*

# Short-Term Effects of Exercise

During exercise, your heart and lungs work extra hard to try and get more oxygen to your muscles so they can work properly. But if your muscles work too hard, they can get a bit tired — poor things.

## There are Short-Term Effects on the Muscular System

1) When you exercise, your muscles release extra energy for movement. Producing this energy also generates heat, which can make you feel hot.
2) Also, during anaerobic activity, your muscles produce lactic acid.
3) If you use your muscles anaerobically for too long, lactic acid starts to build up. This leads to a rise in the lactate levels in the body — lactate accumulation.
4) Lactic acid build-up makes your muscles painful and causes muscle fatigue (tiredness).
5) If your muscles are fatigued, they need oxygen to remove the lactic acid and recover. The amount of oxygen you need is the oxygen debt.
6) To repay oxygen debt, you'll need to slow down or stop the activity you're doing for a while, which can have a negative impact on your performance.
7) During a training session where you do anaerobic activity, you'll need to have periods of rest or low intensity exercise before you can work anaerobically again.

## There are Short-Term Effects on the Respiratory System

1) During exercise, your depth and rate of breathing increase.
2) This means more oxygen is taken in and transferred to the blood, which helps to meet the increased demand for oxygen in the muscles during physical activity.

*Increasing your depth of breathing increases your tidal volume (see p9).*

3) It also helps you to breathe out the extra carbon dioxide produced during aerobic respiration.
4) These changes allow you to do aerobic activity for long periods of time.
5) If you've been doing anaerobic activity, your breathing rate and depth will remain higher than normal until you've taken in enough oxygen to 'pay off' your oxygen debt.

## There are Short-Term Effects on the Cardiovascular System

1) Your heart rate is the number of times your heart beats per minute. An adult's resting heart rate (their heart rate when they aren't exercising) is usually about 60-80 bpm (beats per minute).
2) Your stroke volume is the amount of blood each ventricle pumps with each contraction (or heartbeat).
3) During exercise, your heart rate and stroke volume both increase.
4) This leads to an increase in your cardiac output — the volume of blood pumped by a ventricle per minute.

*cardiac output = heart rate × stroke volume*

5) This increases the blood and oxygen supply to your muscles — so they can release the energy they need for physical activity. It also removes more carbon dioxide from the muscles and takes it to the lungs to be breathed out.
6) Your heart rate, stroke volume and cardiac output will remain higher than normal after exercise until any oxygen debt is paid off.

## My brainular system feels fatigued...

Remember — exercise does more than just make you red-faced and sweaty. Have a go at these Practice Questions.

Q1 Copy and complete the following statements about the short-term effects of exercise.
During exercise, the .................... and stroke volume increase. This leads to an increase in the .................... output so more oxygenated ............... is delivered to the muscles. [3 marks]

Q2 Explain how muscle fatigue may affect a player participating in a game of football. [1 mark]

Section One — Anatomy and Physiology

# Short-Term Effects of Exercise

This page'll show you how the cardiovascular and respiratory systems team up to help you exercise. It'll also give you some handy tips on how to interpret exercise data that you might see in the exam.

## The Cardiovascular and Respiratory Systems Work Together

1) During exercise (and immediately after), more oxygen is delivered to the muscles than normal. Extra carbon dioxide is also taken away from them and breathed out.
2) The cardiovascular and respiratory systems work together to make this happen. When you exercise:

**MORE O₂ DELIVERED**
1) Breathing rate and depth increase, so more oxygen is delivered to the alveoli in the lungs.
2) Cardiac output also increases — so blood passes through the lungs at a faster rate, and picks up the extra oxygen from the alveoli. It's then delivered to the muscles.

**MORE CO₂ REMOVED**
1) Increased cardiac output means that the blood can transport carbon dioxide from the muscles to the lungs more quickly.
2) Here it moves back into the alveoli, and the higher breathing rate and depth allow it to be quickly breathed out.

3) These changes maintain a high concentration gradient — after you breathe in, there's a lot more oxygen in the alveoli than the capillaries, and a lot more carbon dioxide in the capillaries than the alveoli.
4) This allows diffusion of the gases to happen much quicker during exercise.
5) These processes help you to release enough energy to exercise aerobically and to recover from oxygen debt after anaerobic activity (see p11).

*For more on diffusion, have a look at page 8.*

## Short-Term Effects can be shown Graphically

1) In your exam, you might get a graph or table showing someone's heart rate, stroke volume or cardiac output during a workout.
2) These things all increase when you exercise, and gradually go back to normal once you stop exercising.
3) You can use these facts to interpret data and work out whether a person was resting, exercising or recovering at a specific time.

**A** This point is before the person has started exercising. Their heart rate is at its lowest point — it's their resting heart rate.

**B** Their heart rate has started to increase — they've started to exercise.

**C** This part of the graph is when the workout is at its highest intensity. The person's heart rate is at its highest point on the graph.

**D** Their heart rate is decreasing — exercise has stopped, or they're completing a cool down. Their heart rate stays fairly high for a while to help with recovery.

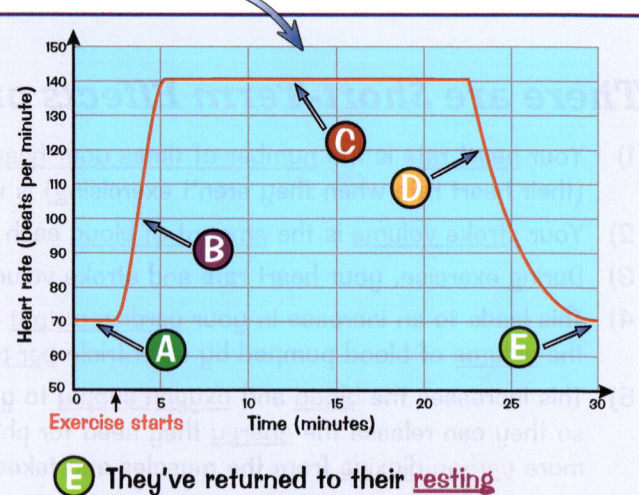

**E** They've returned to their resting heart rate of 70 beats per minute.

## Graphs and tables? I didn't sign up for extra maths lessons...

I bet you weren't pleased to see a graph on this page, but it's not too bad. If you get given any heart rate, stroke volume or cardiac output data in your exam, remember that they all go up during exercise, and back down afterwards. Then you can work out what was going on when the values were recorded. Try this Practice Question.

Q1 The table on the right shows an athlete's stroke volume recorded three times during a training session. Identify which value was recorded:

| 94 cm³ | 141 cm³ | 63 cm³ |

a) before exercise started      [1 mark]      b) during exercise      [1 mark]

Section One — Anatomy and Physiology

# Long-Term Effects of Exercise

Exercising regularly eventually leads to loads of adaptations in the body's systems. These benefit your health and different components of fitness (see pages 19-22), which will help improve your performance.

## Exercise Improves the Musculo-Skeletal System

**MUSCLE HYPERTROPHY**

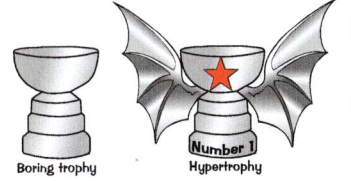

1) Doing regular exercise (especially resistance training) will make your muscles thicker and your muscle girth larger (see p43).
2) This thickening of muscles is called hypertrophy. It happens to all muscles when they're exercised, including your heart.
3) The thicker a muscle is, the more strongly it can contract — so this increases your strength.
4) Hypertrophy also improves your muscular endurance — so you can use your muscles for longer.

*Anaerobic training improves your muscles' ability to work without oxygen.*

**INCREASED BONE DENSITY**

1) The denser your bones, the stronger they are.
2) Exercise usually puts stress or forces through bones, and will cause the body to strengthen those bones.
3) The stronger your bones, the less likely they are to break or fracture.

**STRONGER LIGAMENTS & TENDONS** Having stronger ligaments and tendons means you're less likely to injure yourself, e.g. dislocation (see p32).

## Exercise Improves the Cardio-Respiratory System

**BIGGER/STRONGER HEART**

1) Your heart is just a muscle — when you exercise, it adapts and gets bigger and stronger.
2) A bigger, stronger heart will contract more strongly and pump more blood with each beat — so your resting stroke volume and maximum cardiac output will increase.
3) A larger stroke volume means your heart has to beat less often to pump the same amount of blood around your body. This means your resting heart rate decreases.

**LARGER LUNG CAPACITY**

1) Your diaphragm and external intercostal muscles (the muscles between the ribs) get stronger — so they can make your chest cavity larger.
2) The number of alveoli in your lungs also increases.
3) With a larger chest cavity and more alveoli, your lung capacity increases — you can breathe in more air. This means your vital capacity increases, too.
4) The larger your lung capacity, the more oxygen you can get into your lungs and into your bloodstream per breath.

**LOWER BLOOD PRESSURE**

With regular exercise, your veins and arteries get bigger and their muscular walls become more elastic — so your blood pressure falls.

**MORE CAPILLARIES IN THE MUSCLES**

This increases the blood supply to the muscles, so they receive more oxygen.

**MORE RED BLOOD CELLS**

So the blood can carry more oxygen.

The better the blood and oxygen supply to your muscles, the better your cardiovascular fitness is. This means you can exercise more intensely and for longer, as well as recover more quickly after exercise.

*Training that involves aerobic activity works best to improve the cardio-respiratory system.*

---

### Breaking news — exercise is good for you...

To get all these lovely long-term effects, you'll need to rest after exercise so that you can recover and let your body adapt to any changes. Here's the last Exam Practice Question in this section for you to try. Have fun...

Q1  Explain why muscle hypertrophy would benefit a performer participating in weightlifting.  [3 marks]

Section One — Anatomy and Physiology

# Revision Questions for Section One

Well, that's Anatomy and Physiology all wrapped up — time to see how much you know about the body.
- Try these questions and tick off each one when you get it right.
- When you've done all the questions for a topic and are completely happy with it, tick off the topic.
- The answers can all be found by looking back over pages 1 to 13.

## The Musculo-Skeletal System (p1-5)

1) Name the five main functions of the skeleton.
2) State the four main types of bone in the body.
3) Name the five regions of the vertebral column.
4) Which joint movement involves pointing the toes upwards?
5) Give an example of a condyloid joint.
6) What is the function of:
   a) Cartilage?
   b) Ligaments?
   c) Tendons?
7) Which type of muscle is involved in moving the skeleton — voluntary, involuntary, or cardiac?
8) Which two muscles make up the antagonistic muscle pair operating at the elbow joint?
9) Why would type IIA and IIX muscle fibres not be suitable for use in a marathon?

## The Cardio-Respiratory System (p6-9)

10) What are the three main functions of the cardiovascular system?
11) Which vein does deoxygenated blood pass through to enter the heart?
12) The pulmonary artery carries oxygenated blood to the rest of the body. TRUE or FALSE?
13) Name the three main types of blood vessel found in the body.
14) Explain what vasodilation and vasoconstriction are and why they happen.
15) What is the function of plasma?
16) Explain how oxygen and carbon dioxide are exchanged between the alveoli and capillaries.
17) Give the compositions of inhaled and exhaled air.
18) Describe what is meant by a) tidal volume, and b) vital capacity.

## Aerobic and Anaerobic Exercise (p10)

19) Describe aerobic and anaerobic respiration.
20) What is the main fuel source used in both aerobic and anaerobic activity?

## The Short-Term and Long-Term Effects of Exercise (p11-13)

21) Why do muscles become fatigued during anaerobic activity, and how do they recover?
22) Explain why your depth and rate of breathing increase during exercise.
23) Why do heart rate, stroke volume and cardiac output remain higher after exercise?
24) What is muscle hypertrophy and why does it happen?
25) How does regular exercise benefit the bones, ligaments and tendons?
26) Explain why regular exercise leads to increased oxygen supply to the muscles during exercise.

Section One — Anatomy and Physiology

# Section Two — Movement Analysis

# Lever Systems

When the muscular and skeletal systems work together, they create lever systems that help us to move.

## Lever Systems Help the Body to Move

A lever is a solid bar that moves about a fixed point when force is applied to it.
When a muscle pulls on a bone to move a body part about a joint, it uses the body part as a lever.
This lever makes up part of a lever system that has four different components:

1) The lever arm — the bone or body part being moved about a point.
   On a diagram of a lever system, it's shown as a straight line.
2) The effort — the force applied by the muscles to the lever arm.
   It's shown by an arrow pointing in the direction of the force.
3) The fulcrum — the joint where the lever arm pivots. It's shown as a triangle.
4) The load — the resistance against the pull of the muscles on the lever arm. E.g. the weight of the body, or body part, or something being lifted. A square is used to represent the load.

There are three types of lever system:

**1ST CLASS**
The load and effort are at opposite ends of the lever. The fulcrum is in the middle.
Tilting your head back uses a first class lever.

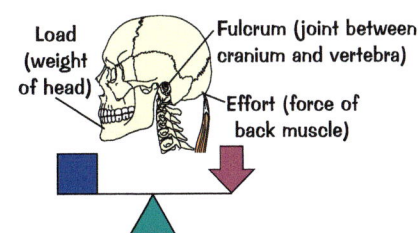

**2ND CLASS**
The fulcrum and effort are at opposite ends of the lever.
The load is in the middle.
Standing on your toes uses a second class lever.

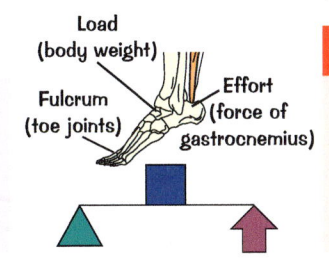

**3RD CLASS**
The fulcrum and load are at opposite ends of the lever.
The effort is in the middle.
Flexion at the elbow (see p3) uses a third class lever.

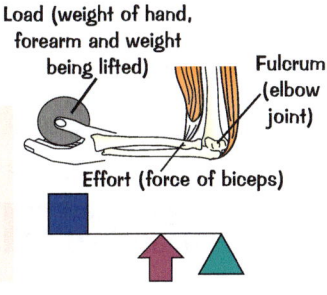

*There aren't many first class levers in the body — third class are the most common.*

## Levers can have a Mechanical Advantage or Disadvantage

Levers help the body use its muscles effectively. Different levers have different benefits — some help to move heavier loads, while others increase the speed a load can be moved at, or the range of movement.

1) A lever in the body with a mechanical advantage can move a large load with a small effort from the muscles. However, it can only move the load short distances at low speeds.

> If the distance from the fulcrum to the effort is greater than the distance from the fulcrum to the load, the lever has a mechanical advantage.

2) Second class levers always have a mechanical advantage — the effort is always further from the fulcrum than the load is.
3) A first class lever has a mechanical advantage if the fulcrum is closer to the load than it is to the effort.
4) A lever with a mechanical disadvantage requires a large effort from the muscles to move a small load — but it can move the load quickly through a large range of movement.
5) Third class levers always have a mechanical disadvantage — the distance from the fulcrum to the effort is always less than the distance from the fulcrum to the load.
6) A first class lever has a mechanical disadvantage if the fulcrum is closer to the effort than it is to the load.

### Moving joints — you'd better lever little space...

To remember the lever classes, use '1, 2, 3, F, L, E'. The letters tell you the middle component of each lever — for 1st class it's the fulcrum, for 2nd class it's the load, and for 3rd class it's the effort. Try this Practice Question.

Q1  State the type of lever system involved in flexion at the knee. [1 mark]

# Planes and Axes of Movement

It might seem a bit odd that there's a page about planes and axes in a PE book — but it'll all make sense soon. Basically, you can describe a body movement using the plane it moves in and the axis it moves around.

## Movements Happen In Planes

1) A plane of movement is an imaginary flat surface which runs through the body.
2) Planes are used to describe the direction of a movement.
3) When you move a body part (or your whole body), it moves in a plane.
4) There are three planes of movement you need to know:

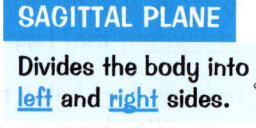

**SAGITTAL PLANE**
Divides the body into left and right sides.

**TRANSVERSE PLANE**
Divides the body into top and bottom.

**FRONTAL PLANE**
Divides the body's front and back.

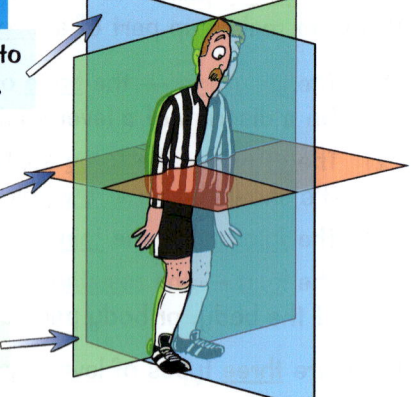

## Movements Happen Around Axes

1) An axis of movement is an imaginary line which runs through the body.
2) When a body part (or your whole body) moves, it moves around (or 'about') an axis.
3) There are three types of axis you need to know:

**SAGITTAL AXIS**
Runs through the body from front to back.

**FRONTAL AXIS**
Runs through the body from left to right.

**VERTICAL AXIS**
Runs through the body from top to bottom.

*If you're talking about more than one axis, they're called 'axes'.*

## Movements use Different Planes and Axes

Every body movement uses both a plane and an axis.
Learn the plane and axis pairs for these movement types and sporting examples.

| MOVEMENT TYPE | PLANE | AXIS | SPORT MOVEMENT |
|---|---|---|---|
| flexion/extension | sagittal | frontal | tucked and piked somersaults |
| abduction/adduction | frontal | sagittal | cartwheel |
| rotation | transverse | vertical | full twist jump (trampolining) |

*Have a look at page 3 for more examples of the movement types.*

*These plane and axis pairs are always the same, e.g. movements that happen in the transverse plane always happen around the vertical axis.*

### Movement in planes — only when the seatbelt signs are off...

Don't forget, you won't see plane and axis combinations different to the ones in the table above — so make sure you learn the pairs for your exam. Once you've done that, have a go at this Exam Practice Question.

Q1  State the plane and axis used during a star jump. [2 marks]

Section Two — Movement Analysis

# Revision Questions for Section Two

Well, Section Two was short and sweet... Try these revision questions to make sure you took it all in.
- Try these questions and tick off each one when you get it right.
- When you've done all the questions for a topic and are completely happy with it, tick off the topic.
- The answers can all be found by looking back over pages 15 and 16.

## Lever Systems (p15)

1) Name the component of a lever system represented by:
    a) a square
    b) a triangle
    c) a straight line
    d) an arrow

2) State the class of each of the levers below.
    a)         b)         c)

3) Which type of lever is most common in the human body?

4) Explain what is meant if a lever system in the body has a:
    a) mechanical advantage
    b) mechanical disadvantage

## Planes and Axes of Movement (p16)

5) What is a plane of movement?

6) Which plane of movement divides:
    a) the top and bottom of the body?
    b) the left and right sides of the body?
    c) the front and back of the body?

7) What is an axis of movement?

8) Which axis runs through the body from:
    a) top to bottom?
    b) front to back?
    c) left to right?

9) Which plane and axis are used during both tucked and piked somersaults? Choose from:
    A  sagittal plane and frontal axis
    B  transverse plane and sagittal axis
    C  frontal plane and sagittal axis
    D  transverse plane and vertical axis

10) Which plane and axis are used during a cartwheel? Choose from:
    A  frontal plane and frontal axis
    B  sagittal plane and sagittal axis
    C  frontal plane and sagittal axis
    D  sagittal plane and frontal axis

11) Which plane and axis are used during a full twist jump in trampolining? Choose from:
    A  transverse plane and vertical axis
    B  sagittal plane and sagittal axis
    C  transverse plane and frontal axis
    D  frontal plane and sagittal axis

Section Two — Movement Analysis

# Section Three — Physical Training

## Health and Fitness

We'll start with telekinesis, then a bit of mind-reading... Sorry, I thought this section was Psychical Training. Try again... First up, four important words: health, fitness, exercise and how they affect performance.

### Fitness is just One Part of being Healthy

1) Being healthy is more than just having a healthy body. Don't take my word for it though — here's the definition used by the World Health Organisation (WHO):

> Health is a state of complete physical, mental and social well-being and not merely the absence of disease or infirmity.

2) Fitness is one part of good health — here's the definition:

> Fitness is the ability to meet the demands of the environment.

So, being fit means you're physically able to do whatever you want or need to do, without getting tired quickly.

3) Fitness helps with physical health, but you can have a high level of fitness without necessarily being physically healthy — e.g. some athletes overtrain and end up getting injured.

4) Mental and social well-being is also part of being healthy — if you're always unhappy, then you're not healthy.

### Exercise Keeps You Fit and Healthy

> Exercise is a form of physical activity done to maintain or improve health and/or fitness.

*It doesn't have to be a competitive sport.*

1) By exercising, you can improve components of fitness (see p19-22) and general physical health.
2) As well as keeping you physically fit, exercise also helps with emotional and social well-being:
   - Exercise is a good stress relief and is enjoyable.
   - Exercise can be a social activity — e.g. joining a yoga class can help you make new friends or socialise with current friends.

*See p37 for more about how exercise helps emotional and social well-being.*

### You need to be Fit and Healthy to Perform Well

1) Your level of health and fitness will affect your performance.

> Performance is how well a task is completed.

2) Your performance won't be as good if you're unfit — e.g. in the second half of a football match you'll get tired and be less effective.
3) Being unhealthy will also affect performance — if you have the flu, playing sport is going to be tricky...

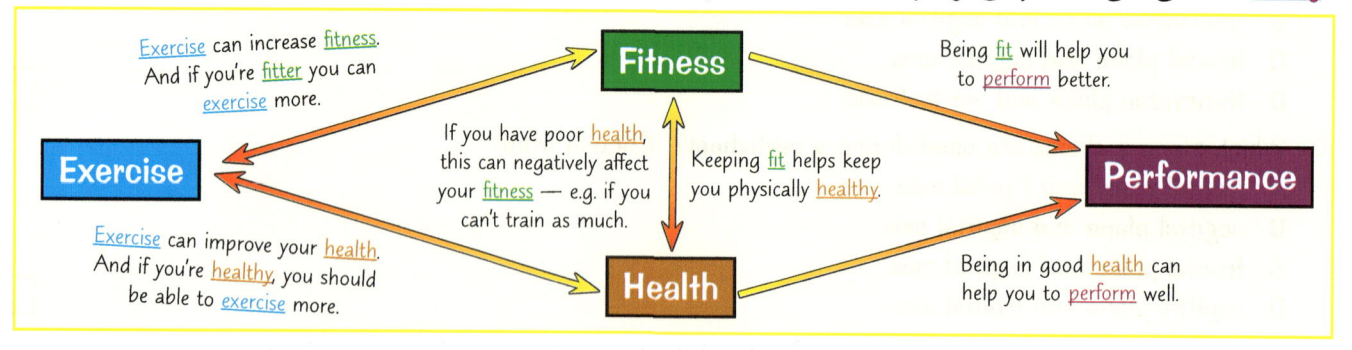

*Alisha was relieved that Gary was fit enough for their performance.*

- Exercise can increase fitness. And if you're fitter you can exercise more.
- If you have poor health, this can negatively affect your fitness — e.g. if you can't train as much.
- Keeping fit helps keep you physically healthy.
- Being fit will help you to perform better.
- Exercise can improve your health. And if you're healthy, you should be able to exercise more.
- Being in good health can help you to perform well.

---

### Health is wealth — you can't buy biscuits with well-being though...

You can see from that rather wonderful diagram (if I say so myself) that these things are all related, and exercise is the key to improving health, fitness and performance. Now, have a go at this Exam Practice Question...

Q1  Explain how an athlete could have a high level of fitness, but still be unhealthy. [2 marks]

Section Three — Physical Training

# Components of Fitness

Fitness can be split up into different components. Six of these components are needed to cope with the physical demands of an activity or sport. Here are the first three, so hop to it and get learning...

## Cardiovascular Fitness — Supplying the Muscles with Oxygen

1) Your heart and lungs work together to keep your muscles supplied with oxygen. The harder you work your muscles, the more oxygen they need.

> CARDIOVASCULAR FITNESS (or AEROBIC ENDURANCE) is the ability of the heart and lungs to supply oxygen to the muscles, so that the whole body can be exercised for a long time.

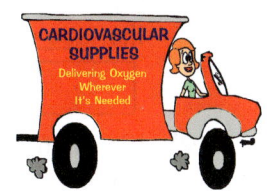

2) So if you have a high level of cardiovascular fitness, your body is able to supply the oxygen your muscles need to do moderately intense whole-body exercise for a long time.
3) Most sports require good cardiovascular fitness. For example, a squash player needs to be able to keep up a fast pace all game. If a tennis player finds they are getting tired and losing points late on in a match, they will want to work on their cardiovascular fitness.
4) A high level of cardiovascular fitness is particularly important for endurance sports like long-distance running, or cycling.

## Strength — the Force a Muscle can Exert

1) Strength is just how strong your muscles are.

> STRENGTH is the amount of force that a muscle or muscle group can apply against a resistance.

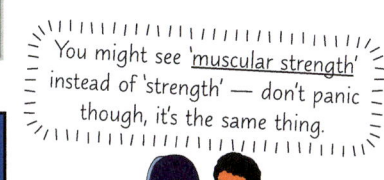

*You might see 'muscular strength' instead of 'strength' — don't panic though, it's the same thing.*

2) It's very important in sports where you need to lift, push or pull things using a lot of force, like weightlifting and judo.
3) Sports that require you to hold your own body weight also need a lot of strength — like the parallel bars and rings in gymnastics.
4) Strength also helps you to do things with power — see p22.

## Muscular Endurance — How Long 'til You get Tired

1) There are two main types of muscle — involuntary and voluntary muscles:

> Involuntary muscles (e.g. the heart) work without any conscious effort from you.
> Voluntary muscles are attached to the skeleton. They're under your control.

*See p4 for more about different muscles.*

2) When your voluntary muscles have been overworked, they get tired and start to feel heavy or weak.

> MUSCULAR ENDURANCE is the ability to repeatedly use the voluntary muscles over a long time, without getting tired.

3) Muscular endurance is really important in any physical activity where you're using the same muscles over and over again — e.g. in racquet sports like tennis or squash where you have to repeatedly swing your arm.
4) It's also dead important towards the end of any long-distance race — rowers and cyclists need muscular endurance for a strong sprint finish.

*Dave's muscular endurance was low — his arm felt heavy after 3 swigs of tea.*

---

### 'Be strong Luke — apply the force against a resistance...'

Make sure you're specific about how components of fitness are used in different activities — e.g. instead of just saying 'strength helps in gymnastics' say 'strength helps the gymnast hold their body weight on the parallel bars'.

Q1 Assess the importance of muscular endurance for a long-distance cyclist. [3 marks]

*Section Three — Physical Training*

# Components of Fitness

Three more components of fitness on this page: flexibility, body composition and speed. Learn what they are — then make sure you learn what sports and activities each one's important in as well. Right, here we go...

## Flexibility — Range of Movement

1) Flexibility is to do with how far your joints move. This depends on the type of joint and the 'stretchiness' of the muscles around it.

> FLEXIBILITY is the amount of movement possible at a joint.

2) It's often forgotten about, but flexibility is dead useful for any physical activity. Here's why...

- **FEWER INJURIES**:
  If you're flexible, you're less likely to pull or strain a muscle or stretch too far and injure yourself.

- **BETTER PERFORMANCE**:
  You can't do some activities without being flexible — e.g. doing the splits in gymnastics.
  Flexibility makes you more efficient in other sports so you use less energy — e.g. swimmers with better flexibility can move their arms further around their shoulders. This makes their strokes longer and smoother.

- **BETTER POSTURE**:
  Bad posture can impair breathing and damage your spine.
  More flexibility means a better posture and fewer aches and pains.

*He'll bend over backwards to help you, you know.*
*So I've heard.*
*It took me years to get this flexible.*

## Body Composition — % of Fat, Muscle and Bone

> BODY COMPOSITION is the percentage of body weight made up by fat, muscle and bone.

1) If you're healthy, your body will normally be made up of between 15% and 25% body fat.
2) Having too much body fat can put strain on your muscles and joints during physical activity.
3) Different activities and sports demand different body compositions, depending on whether you need to be heavy, light, strong, fast, etc.
   - Rock climbers have to be light and strong, so have a high muscle percentage, and a low body fat percentage.
   - In rugby or American football, heavy players have an advantage as they are harder to knock over, so will have a higher body fat percentage than many other sports players.

*Many physical activities become harder to do, and the increased strain on your body means you have a higher risk of injuring yourself.*

## Speed — How Quickly

1) Speed is a measure of how quickly you can do something.
2) This might be a measure of how quickly you cover a distance. It could also be how quickly you can carry out a movement, e.g. how quickly you can throw a punch.
3) To work out speed, you just divide the distance covered by the time taken to do it.
4) Speed is important in lots of activities, from the obvious like a 100 m sprint, to the less obvious (like the speed a hockey player can swing their arm to whack a ball across the pitch).

> SPEED is the rate at which someone is able to move, or to cover a distance in a given amount of time.

---

### I like to think my body composition is 20% fat, 80% hero...

List some sports and then write down the components of fitness that are useful for each sport. I know it's not as fun as playing the sports, but you'll be laughing come exam time. Now, practice makes perfect and all that...

Q1 Give **two** ways that better flexibility can help a swimmer's performance. [2 marks]

Section Three — Physical Training

# Components of Fitness

Now it's time to look at five components of fitness that require skill. Just like the more physical ones, you need to be able to judge their importance for different activities. First up — agility, balance and coordination.

## Agility — Control Over Your Body's Movement

1) Agility is important in any activity where you've got to run about, changing direction all the time, like football or hockey.
2) Jumping and intercepting a pass in netball or basketball involves a high level of agility too.

**AGILITY is the ability to change body position or direction quickly and with control.**

## Balance — More Than Not Wobbling

Having a good sense of balance means you don't wobble or fall over easily. Here's a slightly fancier definition.

**BALANCE is the ability to keep the body's centre of mass over a base of support.**

1) You can think of the mass of any object as being concentrated at just one point. This point is called the centre of mass (or centre of gravity).
2) Everything has a centre of mass — and that includes us.
3) As you change body position, the location of your centre of mass will change too.
4) Whatever activity you're doing, you need to have your centre of mass over whatever is supporting you (your base of support) to balance. If you don't, you'll fall over.

This is true whether you're moving (dynamic balance)...

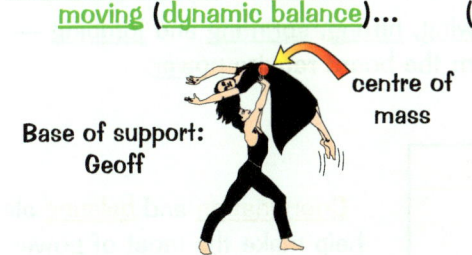

...changing orientation and shape (like in dance and gymnastics)...

...or just staying still (stationary or static balance).

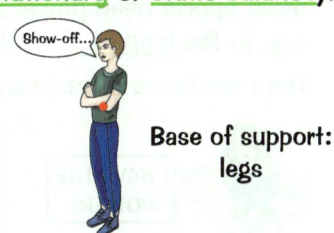

Base of support: Geoff

centre of mass

Base of support: arms

Base of support: legs

5) Balance is crucial for nearly every physical activity. Any sport that involves changing direction quickly — like football or basketball — requires good balance.
6) An action that is performed with balance is more efficient — e.g. a cyclist might work on improving their balance to increase the speed they can go round corners.

## Coordination — Using Body Parts Together

**COORDINATION is the ability to use two or more parts of the body together, efficiently and accurately.**

1) Hand-eye coordination is important in sports that require precision. E.g. being able to hit a ball in tennis, or shoot a bull's-eye in archery.
2) Limb coordination allows you to be able to walk, run, dance, kick, swim...
3) Coordinated movements are smooth and efficient. E.g. a runner with well coordinated arms and legs will be able to run faster than someone who is less coordinated.
4) Limb coordination is really important in sports like gymnastics or platform diving, where your performance is judged on your coordination.

## Agility, Balance and Coordination — as easy as ABC...

Agility, balance and coordination all go together really. You can't be agile if you're not balanced and coordinated. Learn the definitions and how they apply to different activities, then try this Exam Practice Question.

Q1  Explain what is meant by coordination. Give an example of a boxer using coordination. [2 marks]

Section Three — Physical Training

# Components of Fitness

You're nearly there now, just two more components to go. Now you have the agility, balance and coordination of a ninja, what's next? How about cat-like reactions and super power(s)? Sorry, I'm getting carried away...

## Reaction Time — The Time It Takes You to React

> REACTION TIME is the time taken to move in response to a stimulus.

1) In many sports and activities, you need to have fast reactions.
2) The stimulus you respond to could be, e.g., a starter gun, a pass in football, or a serve in tennis.
3) You need fast reactions to be able to hit a ball or dodge a punch.
   It doesn't matter how fast you can move, if you don't react in time you'll miss or get hit.
4) Having fast reactions can effectively give you a head start.

Getting away quickly at the start of a sprint can mean the difference between winning and losing.

Having faster reactions in team sports can help you get away from your opponents, so you can get into better playing positions.

## Power Means Speed and Strength Together

> POWER is a combination of speed and strength.

> power = strength × speed

Most sports need power for some things. It's important for throwing, hitting, sprinting and jumping — e.g. in the long jump, both the sprint run-up and the take-off from the board require power.
Here are some more examples:

I HAVE THE POWER!

| SPORT | YOU NEED POWER TO... |
|---|---|
| Football | ...shoot |
| Golf | ...drive |
| Table tennis | ...smash |
| Tennis | ...serve and smash |
| Cricket | ...bowl fast and bat |

Coordination and balance also help make the most of power — an uncoordinated or off-balance action will not be as powerful.

## Some Components are More Important than Others

1) To be good at any physical activity, you're going to need to have a high level of a number of different components of fitness.
2) For a particular activity, there will always be some components of fitness which are more important than others — e.g. in weightlifting, your strength is more important than your reaction time.
3) To compare the importance of different components, think about the kinds of actions the performer does — e.g. a batsman in cricket has to react to the bowler (reaction time), hit the ball (coordination and power), and then run (speed and cardiovascular fitness).

### Revise more I tell you — sorry, all this power's gone to my head...

Congratulations, you've made it. No more components of fitness to learn. You know the drill — make sure you understand what each component is and which activities it's important in. Then it's Practice Question time.

Q1   Give **two** examples of a player using power in rugby.                    [2 marks]

Section Three — Physical Training

# Fitness Testing

You know what the components of fitness are — now you need to know how to measure them...

## Fitness Testing Helps Identify Strengths and Weaknesses

1) Fitness tests are designed to measure specific components of fitness. It's important you choose the right one for the specific component you're interested in — otherwise the test is meaningless.
2) You can use fitness testing to measure your level of fitness before starting a training programme. The data will show your strengths and weaknesses, so you can plan a personal exercise programme (see p25) that focuses on what you need to improve. Some of the tests are quite demanding, so you need to make sure you are fit enough to manage them.
3) You can carry out fitness tests throughout a training programme to monitor your progress and see whether or not the training you're doing is working.

*Tests need to be carried out using the same procedure each time so comparisons with previous tests are meaningful.*

## Learn how to Carry Out these Fitness Tests...

### HARVARD STEP TEST — CARDIOVASCULAR FITNESS

Equipment needed: stopwatch and 45 cm high step.

1) Do 30 step-ups a minute (a step every two seconds) for 5 minutes.
2) You then take three pulse readings: the first one minute after you finish the test, then two minutes after and then three minutes after.
3) You put these numbers into a formula to work out your score — the higher your score, the fitter you are.

*There are a few different versions of the Harvard step test.*

### COOPER 12-MINUTE RUN AND SWIM TESTS — CARDIOVASCULAR FITNESS

I've only got room to describe the run test here. The swim test's the same, just wetter...

Equipment needed: stopwatch and 400 m track.

1) Run round the track as many times as you can in 12 minutes.
2) The distance you run is recorded in metres. The further you can run, the fitter you are.

### 30 m SPRINT TEST — SPEED

Equipment needed: stopwatch, tape measure and cones to mark the distance.

1) Run the 30 m as fast as you can and record your time in seconds. The fewer seconds, the quicker you are.
2) This test can be done over different distances, e.g. 35 m is often used.

### ILLINOIS AGILITY RUN TEST — AGILITY

Equipment needed: Stopwatch, cones and a tape measure.

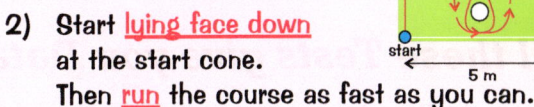

1) Set out a course using cones like this.
2) Start lying face down at the start cone. Then run the course as fast as you can.
3) The course is set up so you have to keep changing direction. The fewer seconds it takes you to finish the course, the more agile you are.

### ONE-MINUTE SIT-UP AND ONE-MINUTE PRESS-UP TESTS — MUSCULAR ENDURANCE

Equipment needed: stopwatch.

1) You just do as many sit-ups or press-ups as you can in a minute.
2) Your result is a number of sit-ups or press-ups per minute — the higher the number, the better your endurance.
3) Sit-ups test your abdominal muscles' endurance. Press-ups test the endurance of your upper body.

### GRIP DYNAMOMETER TEST — STRENGTH

Equipment needed: a dynamometer.

1) A dynamometer is a device used to measure grip strength — the strength in the hand and forearm.
2) You grip as hard as you can for about five seconds and record your reading in kg.
3) Usually, you do it three times and take your best score.

---

### The Harvard staircase test — a step too far...

Make sure that you're clear which test measures which bit of fitness. Now, have a pop at this Practice Question.

Q1 State the component of fitness a grip dynamometer test measures. [1 mark]

Section Three — Physical Training

# Fitness Testing

Two more fitness tests for you to learn here — one measures flexibility and the other measures power. Oh and there's some super fun data stuff too — comparing fitness test scores with average ratings...

## You can also Test your Flexibility and Power

### SIT AND REACH TEST — FLEXIBILITY

Equipment needed: a ruler or tape measure and a box.

1) This test measures flexibility in the back and lower hamstrings.
2) You sit on the floor with your legs straight out in front of you and a box flat against your feet.
3) You then reach as far forward as you can and an assistant measures the distance reached in centimetres — the further you can reach, the more flexible your back and hamstrings are.
4) The distance reached can be measured in different ways — usually it's how many centimetres past your toes that you manage to reach.

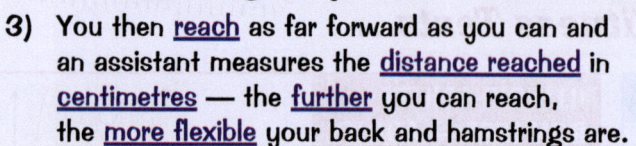

### VERTICAL JUMP TEST — POWER

Equipment needed: chalk, tape measure and a wall.

1) Put chalk on your fingertips and stand side-on to a wall.
2) Raise the arm that's nearest the wall and mark the highest point you can reach.
3) Still standing side-on to the wall, jump and mark the wall as high up as you can.
4) Measure the distance between the marks in centimetres — the larger the distance, the more powerful your leg muscles are.

## All these Tests give you Data about your Fitness levels

Fitness testing gives you a number — e.g. a score, a distance, a time, etc. *These numbers are quantitative data (see p55).*
This is data that you can analyse to assess your fitness levels and make decisions.

1) You can compare your data over time to see how your training is going — e.g. if each week you're recording a bigger distance on the vertical jump test, you know you're increasing your leg power. There's an example of comparing data over time on page 56 — go and have a peek if you like...
2) You can also compare your own performance in a fitness test with average ratings. This can tell you how you rank compared to other people in your age group or gender. *These can be called normative data tables.*
3) Each type of fitness test will have a table that you can compare your results with.

The table below shows average ratings for 16 to 19 year-olds taking the grip dynamometer test. Let's say you want to find the rating for an 18-year-old girl who scored 26 kg:

*'>' means 'greater than', '<' means 'less than'.*

| Gender | Excellent | Good | Average | Fair | Poor |
|---|---|---|---|---|---|
| Male | > 56 kg | 51-56 kg | 45-50 kg | 39-44 kg | < 39 kg |
| Female | > 36 kg | 31-36 kg | 25-30 kg | 19-24 kg | < 19 kg |

① You go down to the correct gender row.
② Then read along to find the range of numbers that includes her score.
③ Finally, go up to see which column this range is in — that gives you the rating.

So, an 18-year-old girl who scored 26 kg on the grip dynamometer test has average grip strength for her gender.

---

### I have a new revision workout for you — number crunches...

Analysing data might be your idea of a living nightmare, but it's key to making sense of all that fitness testing. So, make sure you understand everything on this page. Then do this little Practice Question to check you've got it.

Q1 Sarah scored 5.7 seconds on the 35 m sprint test. Using the data for the 35 m sprint test on the right, which of the following is the correct rating for Sarah?

| Rating | Excellent | Good | Average | Fair | Poor |
|---|---|---|---|---|---|
| Male (seconds) | <4.80 | 4.80-5.09 | 5.10-5.29 | 5.30-5.60 | >5.60 |
| Female (seconds) | <5.30 | 5.30-5.59 | 5.60-5.89 | 5.90-6.20 | >6.20 |

A Excellent      B Good      C Average      D Fair      [1 mark]

Section Three — Physical Training

# Principles of Training

Training isn't about running for as long as possible, or lifting the heaviest weights you can. There's much more to it than that — you need to know how training is matched to different people.

## Train to Improve Your Health, Fitness or Performance

1) To improve your health, fitness or performance, you'll need a Personal Exercise Programme (PEP).
2) A PEP is a training programme designed to improve whatever you want it to improve — it could be your general health and fitness, or a particular component of fitness that will improve your performance in a sport or activity.
3) Different training methods involve different types of exercise and are designed to improve different components of fitness.
4) So you need to choose the right training method. Some key factors to consider will be:

*You will probably have completed a PEP as part of your course...*

What area of your sport or activity you want to improve. You'll need to think about which components of fitness are involved, and which parts of the body too.

*For example, you might want to improve your spike in volleyball.*

What level of fitness you are currently at — you can use fitness testing to find this out. Some methods of training may be too demanding if you are unfit. With any training method, if you're really unfit you'll want to start easy and build up the intensity slowly.

What facilities and equipment you have access to. Some training methods involve lots of specialist equipment and some will also need lots of indoor space.

## SIP — Three Important Principles of Training

When you're planning a training programme, think SIP —
Specificity, Individual needs and Progressive overload:

**S** → SPECIFICITY — matching training to the activity and components of fitness to be developed.
1) You need to train the right parts of the body and in the right way.
2) For example, if a weightlifter wants to get stronger, he or she needs training methods that will focus on increasing muscle strength.

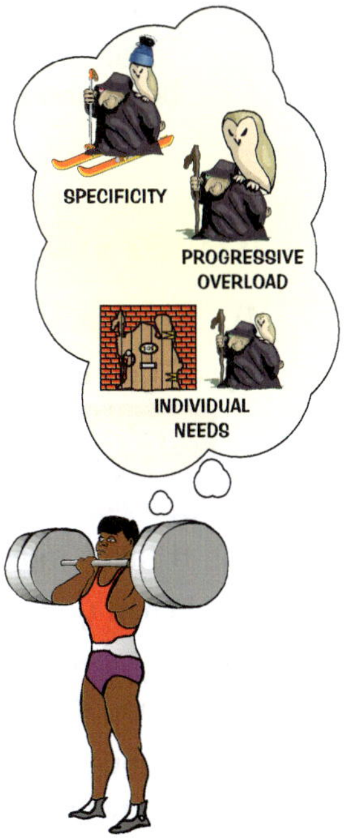

**I** → INDIVIDUAL NEEDS — making training match the needs of an individual.
Every person will need a different training programme — we're all different and we all do different things. Training needs to be done at the right level — if someone's dead unfit, don't start them with a 5-mile swim.

**P** → PROGRESSIVE OVERLOAD — gradually increasing the amount of overload you do to increase your fitness without the injury risk.
1) The only way to get fitter is to work your body harder than it normally would — this is called overload.
2) You can overload by increasing the frequency, intensity or time spent training (see next page).

---

### Put some PEP in your step with a SIP of tea...

The principles of training are tricky, but just remember that the first letter of each principle spells out SIP. Learn everything on this page then try this Exam Practice Question. Oh, and pop the kettle on...

Q1 Explain **one** way in which a rower could apply specificity to their training.  [2 marks]

Section Three — Physical Training

# Principles of Training

The best training programmes aren't just thrown together — they have to be carefully planned. You also have to stick at it — no pumping iron for a week then giving up, else you'll lose everything you've gained.

## Training Programmes can be Planned using FITT

Frequency, Intensity and Time are all part of making sure you overload while you're training.

**F = FREQUENCY of activity — how often you should exercise.**

You can overload by increasing how often you exercise, e.g. gradually increasing the number of training sessions. You need to make sure you leave enough time between sessions to recover though (see below).

**I = INTENSITY of activity — how hard you should exercise.**

How intensely you train depends on your level of fitness and the type of fitness you want to improve. You can overload by gradually increasing intensity — e.g. lifting heavier weights.

**T = TIME spent on activity — how long you should exercise.**

You can overload by gradually increasing the time you spend on a certain exercise or by increasing the overall time spent exercising — e.g. making training sessions five minutes longer each week.

**T = TYPE of activity — what exercises you should use.**

You need to try and match the type of exercise to what it is you're training for — e.g. if you want to improve cardiovascular fitness, you need to do exercise that uses lots of muscles, like running or cycling. Varying types of exercise also helps stop training becoming boring and reduces stress on tissues and joints.

- Your body will begin to change to cope with the increased exercise, so you'll get fitter. These adaptations take place during rest and recovery, so it's vital you allow enough time between training sessions for the body to adapt.
- All training programmes need to be constantly monitored to make sure that the activities are still producing overload. As you get fitter your PEP will need to change to keep improving your fitness.
- It's important that you allow enough recovery time between workouts. Overtraining is when you don't rest enough — it can cause injury by not giving your body enough time to recover from the last training session and repair any damage.

## Reversibility — Keep Training or Your Fitness will Drop

1) You can't train really hard for 4 weeks and get hyper fit, then sit around eating cake for evermore.
2) If you stop training, eventually you'll lose all the fitness you gained — it will reverse.

> **REVERSIBILITY** — any fitness improvement or body adaptation caused by training will gradually reverse and be lost when you stop training.

3) It takes much longer to gain fitness than to lose fitness, which isn't ideal.
4) When you're training, you need to balance your recovery time with the effects of reversibility.
5) If you rest for too long you'll lose most of the benefits of having done the training in the first place. If you don't rest enough you could injure yourself through overtraining.
6) If you get injured, not only have you got to wait for your injury to heal, but thanks to reversibility your fitness will start to decrease while you do. It doesn't seem fair really...

## Revisability — keep revising or your braininess will drop...

Want to be fit? Use **FITT** — Frequency, Intensity, Time and Type. And remember that recovery time is part of training too, because your body needs time to adapt and repair itself. Now, time for another Practice Question...

Q1  Describe what is meant by overtraining. Give **one** way that overtraining could decrease fitness.  [2 marks]

Section Three — Physical Training

# Training Target Zones

To improve aerobic or anaerobic fitness, you need to be training at the right intensity. To work this out, you have to do some calculations based on your heart rate. Nothing like a bit of maths to set the pulse racing...

## Heart Rate — Heartbeats per Minute

1) Your heart rate is the number of times your heart beats per minute (bpm).
2) When you exercise, your heart rate increases to increase the blood and oxygen supply to your muscles. The harder you work, the more your heart rate will increase.
3) You can find your theoretical maximum heart rate (MHR) by doing: **MHR = 220 − Age**
4) And you can use this value to work out how hard you should work to improve you fitness.

*See pages 11-12 for more on how exercise affects your heart rate.*

## Get your Heart Rate in the Target Zone

*Aerobic activity is 'with oxygen' and anaerobic activity is 'without oxygen' — see page 10 for more.*

1) To improve your aerobic or anaerobic fitness, you have to exercise at the right intensity.
2) You can do this by making sure that your heart rate is in a target zone — there are different target zones for aerobic and anaerobic training:

**AEROBIC TARGET ZONE —** 60%-80% of maximum heart rate.

**ANAEROBIC TARGET ZONE —** 80%-90% of maximum heart rate.

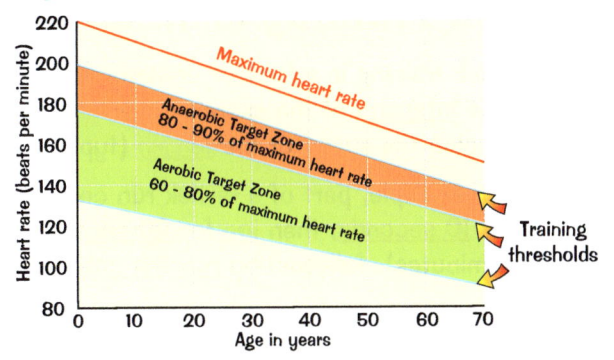

3) The boundaries of the training zones are called training thresholds. If you're a beginner, you should train nearer the lower threshold. Serious athletes train close to the upper threshold.

## Calculating Target Zones — Example

Let's say you want to work out the aerobic target zone for a 20-year-old:

1) First, you calculate their maximum heart rate by subtracting their age from 220 — that's 220 − 20 = 200.
2) Next you find the thresholds. Because you're calculating the aerobic target zone, the lower threshold is 60% of the maximum heart rate — that's 200 × 0.6 = 120. The upper threshold is 80% of the maximum heart rate — so 200 × 0.8 = 160.
3) So the target zone for aerobic training is between 120 and 160 beats per minute.

*For the anaerobic thresholds, you'd use 0.8 and 0.9.*

## Your Training Intensity Should Suit Your Activity

1) If you want to be good at an aerobic activity, like long-distance running, then you should do a lot of aerobic activity as part of your training.
2) Anaerobic training helps your muscles put up with lactic acid. They also get better at getting rid of it. For anaerobic activity like sprinting, you need to do anaerobic training.
3) In many team sports, like lacrosse, you need to be able to move about continuously (aerobic), as well as needing to have spurts of fast movement (anaerobic). You should have a mix of aerobic and anaerobic activities in your training for these.

*Aerobike training*

---

### I did a workout at a camp site — that was training in tent city...

Make sure you know the percentages that go with aerobic and anaerobic target zones. Keep practising working out different target zones — the more you do it now, the easier it'll be in the exam. Speaking of practice...

Q1 Calculate the lower threshold of the anaerobic training zone for a 35-year-old. [3 marks]

Section Three — Physical Training

# Training Methods

Next up, training methods. Remember, you have to match the type of training with what you are training for.

## Continuous Training Means No Resting

1) Continuous training involves exercising at a constant rate, doing activities like running or cycling for at least 20 minutes with no breaks.
2) It improves cardiovascular fitness and muscular endurance, and is great for body composition as well.
3) It usually means exercising so that your heart rate is in your aerobic training zone (see p27). This means it's good training for aerobic activities like long-distance running.
4) Overload is achieved by increasing the duration, distance, speed or frequency.

**ADVANTAGES:**
- It's easy to do — going for a run doesn't require specialist equipment.
- Not resting helps prepare for sports where you have to play for long periods of time without a break.

*After six years of continuous training surely I deserve a rest...*

**DISADVANTAGES:**
- It only involves aerobic activity so doesn't improve anaerobic fitness.
- It can become boring doing one exercise at a constant rate.

## Fartlek Training is all about Changes of Speed

1) Fartlek training is a type of continuous training, but it involves changes in the intensity of the exercise over different intervals — e.g. by changing the speed or the terrain (type or steepness of the ground).

   For example, part of a fartlek run could be to sprint for 10 seconds, then jog for 20 seconds (repeated for 4 minutes), followed by running uphill for 2 minutes.

2) It's great for cardiovascular fitness and muscular endurance and also helps to improve speed.
3) You can include a mix of aerobic and anaerobic activity, so it's good training for sports that need different paces, like hockey and rugby.
4) Overload is achieved by increasing the times or speeds of each bit, or the terrain difficulty (e.g. running uphill).

**ADVANTAGE:**
- It's very adaptable, so you can easily tailor training to suit different sports and different levels of fitness.

**DISADVANTAGE:**
- Frequent changes to intensity can mean that training lacks structure — this makes it easy to skip the hard bits and tough to monitor progress.

## Interval Training uses Fixed Patterns of Exercise

1) Interval training uses fixed patterns of periods of high intensity exercise and either low intensity exercise or rest. It has a strict structure.

   *Interval training can be adapted for lots of different sports — like swimming, rowing and cycling.*

2) By combining high and low intensity work, interval training allows you to improve both cardiovascular fitness and anaerobic fitness. The high intensity periods can also improve speed.
3) It's great training for sports where you have to move continuously (aerobic), then have sudden spurts of fast movement (anaerobic) — like rugby or water polo.
4) To overload you have to increase the proportion of time spent on the high intensity exercise, or the intensity — e.g. run faster.

**ADVANTAGE:**
- It's easily adapted to improve aerobic or anaerobic fitness by changing the intensity and length of work and recovery periods.

**DISADVANTAGE:**
- Interval training is exhausting. This can make it difficult to carry on pushing yourself.

*Nige's interval training: run for 1 minute, bathe for 30 minutes, and repeat...*

---

**Fartlek training —** ............................................................ (Add your own joke.)

Once you're done admiring your own wit, there's an Exam Practice Question with your name on it...

**Q1** Explain why continuous training is better training for a marathon than for a 100 m sprint. **[4 marks]**

Section Three — Physical Training

# Training Methods

*Resistance training* helps you to get stronger, *circuit training* lets you do lots of different exercises in one go.

## *Resistance Training* Helps *Strength* and *Muscular Endurance*

Resistance training means using your muscles against a resistance. Often weights are used as the resistance, so you might also see it called weight training. You can also use elastic ropes as resistance, or your own body weight — like in a pull-up or press-up.

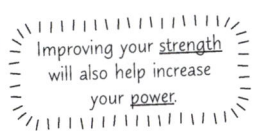

*Improving your strength will also help increase your power.*

1) Resistance training can be used to develop strength and muscular endurance.
2) It's anaerobic training, so is good for improving performance in anaerobic activities like sprinting.
3) Increasing strength/power means you can hit or kick something harder (hockey, football), throw further (javelin, discus), sprint faster, out-muscle opposition (judo), etc.
4) There are two ways to do resistance training:

You can train by contracting your muscles to create movement. Each completed movement is called a 'rep' (repetition), and a group of reps is called a 'set'.

**Example**: BICEPS CURLS
Raise a dumbbell up to your chest and back down again.

- To increase muscular endurance, you use low weight but a high number of reps. To overload, gradually increase the number of reps.
- To increase strength you use high weight but a low number of reps. To overload, gradually increase the weight — but decrease the reps to avoid injury.

You can train by increasing the tension in a muscle, without changing the muscle's length (so there's no movement).

**Example**: THE WALL SIT
Sit with your back to the wall and your knees bent at 90° and hold it.

You overload by staying in the position for longer, or holding weights while you're in the position.

**ADVANTAGES:**
- It's easily adapted to suit different sports — you can focus on the relevant muscles.
- Many of the exercises (press-ups, sit-ups, etc.) require very little equipment to do.

**DISADVANTAGE:**
- It puts muscles under high stress levels, so can leave them very sore afterwards.

## *Circuit Training* Uses *Loads of Different Exercises*

Each circuit has between 6 and 10 'stations' in it. At each station you do a specific exercise for a set amount of time before moving on to the next station.

1) A circuit's stations can work on aerobic or anaerobic fitness — e.g. star jumps for cardiovascular fitness, tricep dips for strength, shuttle runs for speed, etc.
2) You're allowed a short rest between stations. An active rest, e.g. jogging instead of stopping exercising, will improve cardiovascular fitness.
3) Overload is achieved by doing more repetitions at each station, completing the circuit more quickly, resting less between stations, or by repeating the circuit.

**DISADVANTAGE:**
- It takes a long time to set up and requires loads of equipment and space.

**ADVANTAGES:**
- Because you design the circuit, you can match circuit training to an individual and any component of fitness — e.g. you can improve muscular endurance, strength, cardiovascular fitness... anything you want really.
- Also, the variety keeps the training interesting.

## *I prefer wait training myself — far less strenuous...*

Make sure that you understand how resistance training can help with both muscular endurance and strength. For endurance do low weight, high reps. For strength do high weight, low reps. Keep saying it over and over...

Q1 Explain how an athlete can train using weights to improve their strength. [2 marks]

*Section Three — Physical Training*

# Training Methods

Right, last page of training methods, I promise... Plyometrics helps make you more powerful. Fitness classes are a good way to make exercising sociable and maybe even a little bit fun...

## Plyometric Training Improves Power

Loads of sports require explosive strength and power (see p22), e.g. for fast starts in sprinting, or sports where you need to jump high, like basketball or volleyball. You can train muscular power using plyometrics.

1) During movement, muscles can either shorten or lengthen.
2) If a muscle lengthens just before it shortens, it can help to generate power. When a muscle gets stretched and lengthens, extra energy is stored in the muscle (like storing energy in an elastic band by stretching it). This extra energy means the muscle can generate a greater force when it shortens.
3) The extra energy doesn't last very long though. So, the quicker your muscles can move between the lengthening and shortening phases, the more powerful the movement will be.
4) Plyometric training improves the speed you can switch between the two phases, so it improves your power. It's anaerobic exercise and often involves jumping.

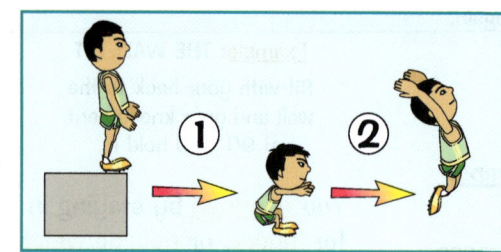

Depth jumps are a form of plyometric training. They improve the power of your quadriceps and increase how high you can jump. You drop off a box then quickly jump into the air. The first stage lengthens your quadriceps as you land and squat, the second stage shortens them as you jump.

**ADVANTAGE:**
- It's the only form of training that directly improves your power.

**DISADVANTAGE:**
- It's very demanding on the muscles used — you need to be very fit to do it, otherwise you'll get injured.

## Fitness Classes make Training More Social and More Fun

As well as all those training methods, there's a host of activities and classes that help improve fitness. Classes can also make training a more social experience.

**AEROBICS** — This involves doing aerobic exercises to music. It's good for improving cardiovascular fitness, strength and flexibility.

**YOGA AND PILATES** — Both yoga and Pilates use a series of exercises and stretches that help increase strength, flexibility and balance. Both help to prevent injury as well as making you fitter.

*Yoga exercises the whole body, while Pilates focuses more on the core torso muscles, e.g. the abdominals.*

**BODYPUMP™** — This is a choreographed workout that combines weight training and aerobics. It's good for improving strength, muscular endurance and cardiovascular fitness.

**SPINNING®** — This is a high intensity workout using exercise bikes which can be set to different levels of resistance by participants. It's good for improving both your cardiovascular and anaerobic fitness.

Using any of the training methods covered on the last three pages over a period of time has long-term effects on the body systems. By improving components of fitness, you can improve the performance of the musculo-skeletal and cardio-respiratory systems — see page 13 for the details. These changes have a positive effect on both your health and performance in physical activity and sport.

### So many fitness classes to learn — my head is spinning...

That's it — you've made it to the end of training methods, phew. Remember that games players will still need to practise skills and actions that are specific to their sport, as well as improving relevant components of fitness.

Q1 Justify why a basketball player would train using plyometrics. [3 marks]

Section Three — Physical Training

# Preventing Injuries

With any physical activity there's always a risk of injury. You need to know how to make it as safe as possible.

## PARQ — Physical Activity Readiness Questionnaire

1) PARQs are made up of 'yes or no' questions, designed to assess whether it's safe for you to increase your physical activity.
2) It's a good idea to fill one in before you start a training programme.
3) If you answer yes to any of the questions, you need to visit your doctor to make sure it's safe first. This could also lead to changes in the programme to make sure it's safe for you to participate.

**PARQ** — Yes / No
- Have you ever been diagnosed with a heart problem?
- Are you currently being prescribed any medication?
- Do you have any problems with your joints?

## To Avoid Injury do These Four Things...

*You need to be able to apply these factors to different activities and sports.*

### CHECK EQUIPMENT/FACILITIES
- Use the right equipment — and check it's not damaged and is in good condition.
- Check for possible dangers in the area you're going to be exercising in — e.g. glass hidden in the grass on a football pitch, or slippery patches caused by bad weather on a running track.

### PLAY BY THE RULES
- Know and follow the rules of the game. Some rules are there to help stop injuries — e.g. giving yellow or red cards for bad tackles in football.
- Use the correct technique — e.g. tackling safely in rugby, or safely lifting weights in weight training.
- Use officials (e.g. a referee) to ensure there's fair play and the rules are followed.

### USE THE CORRECT CLOTHING/EQUIPMENT
- Make sure you're not wearing anything that could get caught (e.g. jewellery, watches).
- Wear suitable footwear — e.g. wearing studded football boots or spiked running shoes will make you less likely to slip and injure yourself.
- Use protective clothing/equipment where appropriate — e.g. gum shields, cycling helmets.

### STRUCTURE TRAINING CORRECTLY
- Follow the Principles of Training (see p25-26).
- This means not overdoing it — you need to allow time for rest and recovery, otherwise you can get overuse injuries. Also, make sure the intensity of exercise matches your level of fitness.

## ...And always Warm Up First and Cool Down Afterwards

### WARM-UP
Gets your body ready for exercise by gradually increasing your work rate. There are three main phases:
1) Raising your pulse — light exercise increases your heart rate and gets blood flowing to the muscles.
2) Stretching — this increases flexibility at your joints — so you're ready for the work and less likely to injure yourself. The stretches should focus on the muscles you will use in the activity.
3) Practice actions — e.g. practice shots in netball. This prepares the muscles that are going to be used.

Practice actions also help prepare you mentally by concentrating your mind on the activity. You can also visualise what you need to do (see p45).

### COOL-DOWN
Gets your body back to normal after exercise by gradually decreasing the intensity of work to control your return to resting levels.
1) Gentle exercise like jogging keeps the heart and lungs working:
   - This means you can take in enough oxygen to get rid of the lactic acid in your muscles.
   - This also helps keep the blood flowing back from the muscles, so stops blood pooling in the legs and arms — blood pooling can cause dizziness and even fainting.
2) Stretching can help to reduce muscle soreness later on.

---

### All this talk of injuries is making my brain hurt...
Warming up is especially important for more intense, anaerobic activities, where it's easy to get an injury.

Q1 Evaluate the importance of a pre-match warm-up in helping a hockey player to avoid injury. [9 marks]

Section Three — Physical Training

# Injuries and Treatment

Now for the gruesome bit — injuries. As my grandma used to say, 'It's all fun and games until someone gets hurt.' And she would know — she's a prize-winning cage-fighter...

## Soft Tissues can get Stretched, Ripped and Torn

Soft tissues are skin, muscles, tendons and ligaments. Basically, all the bits of you that aren't bone...

### Damage to the Skin is Common in Sport

1) Grazes, blisters and chafing are all types of abrasion. They can break the skin and cause bleeding.
2) Cuts also damage the skin and cause bleeding. A deep cut will damage the tissue beneath the skin as well. Deep cuts like this will require medical attention.
3) Injuries to the skin can occur in most physical activities, although they're especially common in full-contact sports like rugby or boxing.

### Strains are Tears in Muscles or Tendons

1) Strained (pulled) muscles and tendons are tears in the tissue. They're often caused by sudden overstretching.
2) Pulled hamstrings and calf muscles are common injuries in sports like football and cricket, where you use sudden bursts of speed.

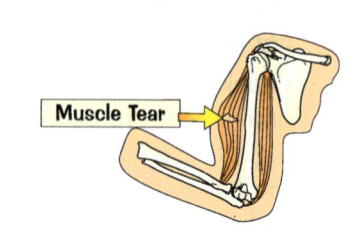

*Muscle Tear*

### Sprains are Damage to Ligaments

1) Sprains are joint injuries where the ligament has been stretched or torn, usually because of violent twisting.
2) These types of injuries are common in sports where players have to change direction quickly, like football and basketball.

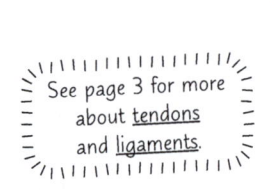

*See page 3 for more about tendons and ligaments.*

## Some Injuries are Caused by Continuous Stress...

Continuous stress on part of the body over a long period of time can cause all sorts of problems:

1) Tennis players can develop tennis elbow — painful inflammation of tendons in the elbow due to overuse of certain arm muscles.
2) Golfers get a similar injury called, wait for it... golfer's elbow.
3) You're more at risk of this type of injury if you train too hard or don't rest enough between training sessions.
4) As these are injuries to tendons, they are also types of soft-tissue injury.

## ...others by Sudden Stress

1) Cartilage can be damaged by sudden movements.
2) E.g. the cartilage of the knee can be torn by a violent impact or twisting motion.
3) Joints can get dislocated as well.
4) The bone is pulled out of its normal position — again, it's twisting that usually does it.
5) This can damage the ligaments, muscles and tendons around the joint too.

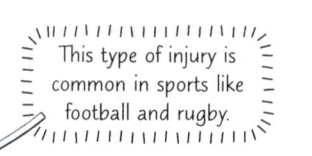

*This type of injury is common in sports like football and rugby.*

*See page 3 for more about cartilage.*

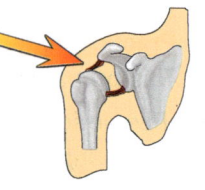

**Dislocated shoulder** — Humerus pulled out of joint.

---

### Sprains, Strains and Automobiles...

It's easy to get sprains and strains mixed up. So, write down 'a strain is a muscle or tendon injury' over and over until it's lodged nice and firmly in your brain. And now, free cake... (Not really, just another Exam Practice Question.)

Q1  Name the soft tissue damaged in a sprain. [1 mark]

Section Three — Physical Training

# Injuries and Treatment

My grandma isn't really a cage-fighter — that was a lie. She does make a mean rice pudding though. You can treat injuries using the RICE method — Rest, Ice, Compression and Elevation. Neat huh?

## Broken Bones are Called Fractures

1) A fracture is a break in a bone. It's usually accompanied by bruising and swelling.
2) This is because a fracture also damages the blood vessels in or around the bone.
3) It'll also cause a lot of pain because of the damaged nerves inside the bone.
4) There are four types of fracture you need to know:

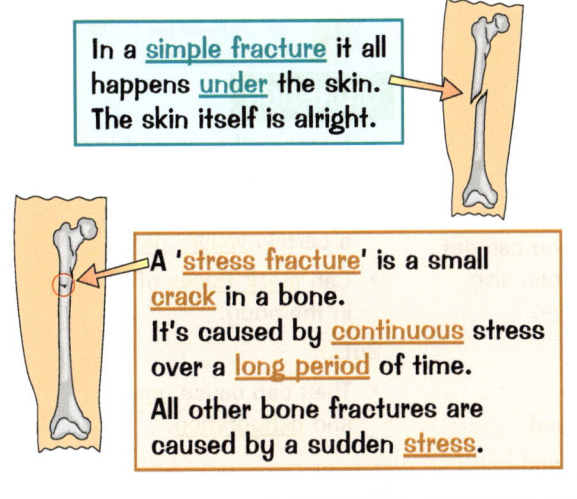

In a simple fracture it all happens under the skin. The skin itself is alright.

In a compound fracture the skin is torn and the bone pokes out. Urgghh.

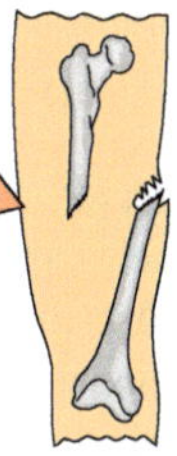

A 'stress fracture' is a small crack in a bone. It's caused by continuous stress over a long period of time. All other bone fractures are caused by a sudden stress.

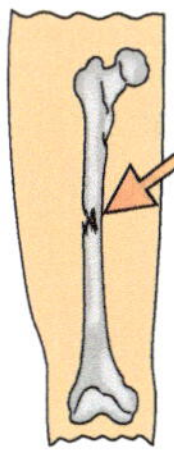

Greenstick fractures happen in young or soft bone that bends and partly breaks.

## Concussion is Caused by a Blow to the Head

1) A concussion is a mild brain injury caused by a nasty blow to the head.
2) The symptoms of concussion are: disorientation, memory loss and possibly loss of consciousness.
3) If someone with concussion is unconscious, check they've not injured their neck or spine, then place them in the recovery position (with the head tilted so the airway won't be blocked by the tongue or by vomit) and get an ambulance. If they're conscious, keep them under observation for at least 48 hours.

## Use the RICE Method to Treat Injuries

| R | REST | ➡ | Stop immediately and rest the injury — if you carry on, you'll make it worse. |
| I | ICE | ➡ | Apply ice to the injury. This makes the blood vessels contract to reduce internal bleeding and swelling. |
| C | COMPRESSION | ➡ | Bandaging the injury will also help reduce swelling. But don't make it so tight that you stop the blood circulating altogether. |
| E | ELEVATION | ➡ | Support the limb at a raised level (i.e. above the heart). The flow of blood reduces because it has to flow against gravity. |

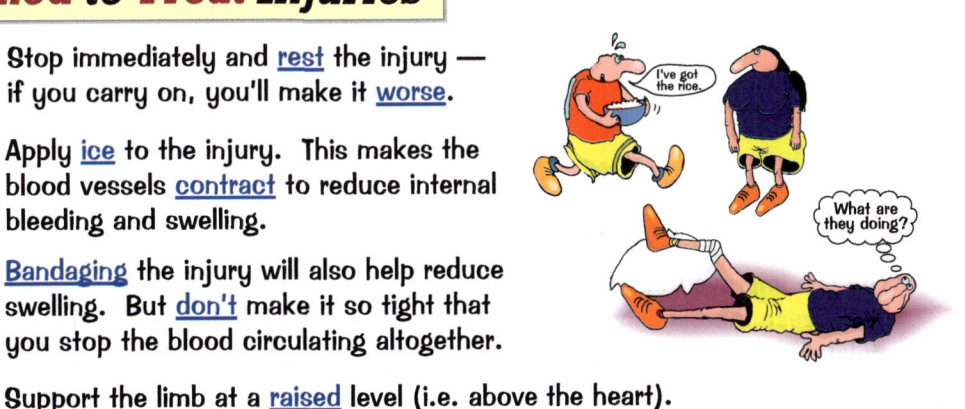

The RICE method is a good treatment for joint and muscle injuries like sprains or strains. It reduces pain, swelling and bruising. But, if there's an injury to the neck or spine, it's best not to move the person.

### If the RICE treatment doesn't work, try the noodles...

What a pair of really nasty pages. With all the bones, and the breaking... Lots of stuff to know here — no way around it I'm afraid, so get memorising. Then it's time for another Exam Practice Question methinks.

Q1  Explain how to treat a sprained ankle.  [2 marks]

Section Three — Physical Training

# Performance-Enhancing Drugs

Some people cheat by taking drugs. Drugs can help them perform better, but they can also cause serious health problems. You need to know the positive and negative effects of these drugs on the performer...

## Performance-Enhancing Drugs can Improve Performance

1) Some athletes use drugs to improve their performance and be more successful in their sport. The use of these drugs in sport is usually banned, and they can have nasty side effects.

2) Unfortunately, some athletes still break the rules by taking them anyway — even with the risks to their health and reputation if they're caught. These are the drugs you need to know about:

*Taking performance-enhancing drugs is a form of deviance (see p53).*

*Now, which one of you gentlemen has been taking steroids?*

### BETA BLOCKERS
- Are drugs that control heart rate.
- They lower the heart rate, steady shaking hands, and have a calming, relaxing effect.

But...
- They can cause nausea, low blood pressure, cramp and heart failure.

### STIMULANTS
- Affect the central nervous system (the bits of your brain and spine that control your reactions).
- They can increase mental and physical alertness.

But...
- They can lead to high blood pressure, heart and liver problems, and strokes.
- They're addictive.

### ANABOLIC STEROIDS
- Mimic the male sex hormone testosterone.
- Testosterone increases your bone and muscle growth (so you can get bigger and stronger). It can also make you more aggressive.

But...
- They cause high blood pressure, heart disease, infertility and cancer.
- Women may grow facial and body hair, and their voice may deepen.

### NARCOTIC ANALGESICS
- Kill pain — so injuries and fatigue don't affect performance so much.

But...
- They're addictive, with unpleasant withdrawal symptoms.
- Feeling less pain can make an athlete train too hard.
- They can lead to constipation and low blood pressure.

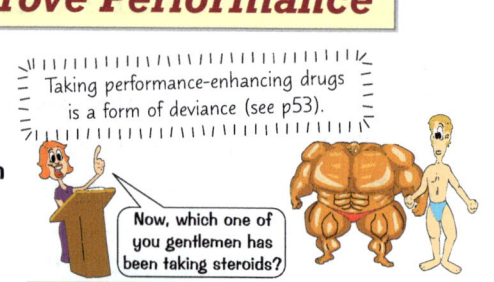

### DIURETICS
- Increase the amount you urinate, causing weight loss — important if you're competing in a certain weight division.
- Can mask traces of other drugs in the body.

But...
- They can cause cramp and dehydration.

### PEPTIDE HORMONES
- Cause the production of other hormones — similar to anabolic steroids.
- EPO (Erythropoietin) is a peptide hormone that causes the body to produce more red blood cells.
- GH (Growth Hormones) are peptide hormones that make the body build more muscle.

But...
- They can cause strokes and heart problems. GH can also cause abnormal growth and diabetes.

## Blood Doping is Banned

You can improve your performance by increasing the number of red blood cells in your bloodstream to increase the oxygen supply to your muscles. Blood doping is a form of cheating that increases an athlete's number of red blood cells unfairly. It can be done in one of two ways:

1) Before a competition an athlete can be injected with red blood cells. Possible side effects of injecting red blood cells include allergic reactions, kidney damage and blocked capillaries or, if the blood is from someone else, catching viruses such as HIV.

2) Athletes can also take EPO to increase their red blood cell count (see peptide hormones above).

---

### Cheating — it's just not worth it...

A trick for remembering these: think BADSNAP — (Beta blockers, Anabolic steroids, Diuretics, Stimulants, Narcotic Analgesics, Peptide hormones). Now, guess what? That's right, Exam Practice Question time...

Q1  Identify **one** performance-enhancing drug that an archer might use. Explain your choice.  [2 marks]

Section Three — Physical Training

# Revision Questions for Section Three

So, it turns out there's more to physical training than montages, slow motion and cheesy power ballads...
- Try these questions and tick off each one when you get it right.
- When you've done all the questions for a topic and are completely happy with it, tick off the topic.
- The answers can all be found by looking back over pages 18 to 34.

## Health and Fitness (p18)
1) What is the definition of fitness?
2) What is the definition of performance?
3) Give two ways that exercise can help keep you healthy.

## Components of Fitness (p19-22)
4) What is cardiovascular fitness?
5) Is muscular endurance needed to repeatedly use voluntary or involuntary muscles?
6) Define flexibility. Give one benefit of increased flexibility for an athlete.
7) Describe coordination. How does having good coordination help a sprinter?
8) What is power? Give an example of when power would be needed in golf.

## Fitness Testing (p23-24)
9) Describe the Harvard step test. Which component of fitness does it measure?
10) Which component of fitness does the sit and reach test measure? What units are the results in?
11) Outline a fitness test that measures: a) speed, b) power, c) muscular endurance.

## Training (p25-30)
12) Name three important principles of training.
13) What are the three ways that overload can be achieved in training?
14) What are the four principles of FITT?
15) Describe how to calculate your anaerobic target zone.
16) Does continuous training improve anaerobic fitness?
17) Describe the fartlek training method. Give an advantage and a disadvantage.
18) How is overload achieved in circuit training?
19) Which component of fitness does plyometric training improve?

## Injuries and Treatment (p31-33)
20) What does PARQ stand for? Should it be used before or after a training programme?
21) How many phases should a warm-up have? Outline each of the phases.
22) Name the soft tissue damaged in: a) an abrasion, b) a sprain, c) a strain.
23) Give three symptoms of a concussion.
24) What does RICE stand for? Give two types of injury that can be treated with the RICE method.

## Performance-Enhancing Drugs (p34)
25) Describe the positive and negative effects of: a) beta blockers, b) diuretics, c) stimulants.
26) Outline two methods of blood doping. What are the health risks involved in each method?

Section Three — Physical Training

# Health, Fitness and Well-being

Regular physical activity helps you to be healthy by improving your physical, emotional and social health and well-being. First up, the obvious one — exercise helps keep you physically healthy...

## If your Body Works Well, you are Physically Healthy

1) Physical health and well-being is an important part of being healthy and happy.
2) Taking part in sport or other physical activities has loads of physical benefits.

*See p13 for more about how exercise benefits your body systems.*

**PHYSICAL HEALTH AND WELL-BEING:**

1) Your body's organs, e.g. the heart, and systems, e.g. the cardiovascular system, are working well.
2) You're not suffering from any illnesses, diseases or injuries.
3) You're strong and fit enough to easily do everyday activities.

1) By exercising you can improve components of fitness (see p19-22), which benefits your physical health:
- Aerobic exercise improves your cardiovascular fitness — your heart, blood vessels and lungs work better, and your blood pressure decreases.
- Exercise can benefit your musculo-skeletal system — muscles and bones get stronger, and joints more flexible.
- Exercise can improve body composition — you can attain a healthy weight, which reduces strain on your body.

2) These positive effects on the body reduce the risk of obesity and other long-term health problems (see below). Stronger muscles and more flexible joints can make injury less likely.

3) Physical activity makes you stronger and fitter — so everyday tasks like climbing stairs and lifting shopping are easier. It's not all good though — overtraining (see p26) can have a negative effect on your health.

*Now that's what I call shoplifting.*

## Exercise Reduces Risks to Long-Term Health

Regular physical activity can help reduce the risks of you getting certain diseases. For example:

1) Regular aerobic exercise helps prevent high blood pressure by keeping your heart strong and arteries elastic, and helping to remove cholesterol from artery walls.
2) This means blood can flow easily round the body, which reduces the risk of coronary heart disease, strokes and damage to your arteries.

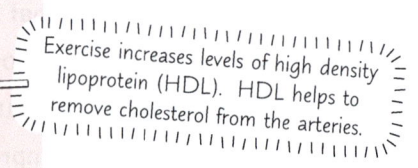

*Exercise increases levels of high density lipoprotein (HDL). HDL helps to remove cholesterol from the arteries.*

Weight-bearing exercise can help to prevent osteoporosis. Osteoporosis is a disease where your bones become fragile. Weight-bearing exercise, where your legs and feet support your whole body weight (like aerobics or running), helps to strengthen your bones.

Regular exercise helps prevent obesity. Exercise uses up energy, meaning that your body doesn't store it as fat (see p39).

*I'm not sure we've got this quite right...*

Type-2 diabetes is a disease that gives you a high blood sugar level. Your blood sugar level is controlled by a hormone called insulin. If you have diabetes, this means you don't have enough insulin or your body's cells aren't reacting to insulin properly (they're insulin-resistant).
Regular exercise helps you avoid diabetes in two ways:
1) Regular exercise helps you maintain a healthy weight. This makes you far less likely to get diabetes.
2) Regular exercise helps improve how sensitive to insulin your cells are. This means you are less likely to become insulin-resistant.

---

### All these benefits of exercise and I'm sitting around writing jokes...

There are so many benefits to exercise it's easy to forget that it can also have a negative effect on your physical health through overtraining... Here's an Exam Practice Question for you, because I know how much you love 'em.

Q1 Explain **one** way that regular exercise helps to prevent type-2 diabetes. [2 marks]

# Health, Fitness and Well-being

As well as making you into a Schwarzenegger-like picture of physical health, exercise is great for your emotional and social health. You need to be able to give examples of how it helps.

## Emotional Health is about how you Feel

1) Being healthy is more than just having a body that works well — you also have to take into account how you feel. Your emotional health and well-being is based on how you feel about yourself and how you respond to different situations.
2) Taking part in physical activity and sport can have emotional benefits:

*Emotional health can also be called 'psychological health'.*

**EMOTIONAL HEALTH AND WELL-BEING:**
1) You feel content and confident in yourself.
2) You are able to manage your emotions and cope with challenges.
3) You don't have too much stress or anxiety.
4) You're not suffering from any mental illnesses.

1) Physical activity can increase your self-esteem (your opinion of yourself) and confidence, and generally make you feel better about yourself — e.g. if you feel you've achieved something.

2) Competing against others (or yourself) can improve your ability to deal with pressure and manage emotions.

3) Doing physical activity can help relieve stress and tension by taking your mind off whatever's worrying you and by making you feel happier. This helps prevent stress-related illnesses.

4) When you do physical activity, the level of endorphins in your brain increases. Endorphins help you to feel good, which can reduce the risk of mental illnesses like depression. Exercise also increases the level of serotonin in your brain. This may help reduce the risk of mental illness, as low levels of serotonin are connected with depression.

## Social Health is about how you Relate to Society

1) Your social health and well-being is about how you interact with others and form relationships.
2) There can be plenty of social benefits from doing physical activity and sport:

**SOCIAL HEALTH AND WELL-BEING:**
1) You have friends.
2) You believe you have some worth in society.
3) You have food, clothing and shelter.

1) Doing physical activity can help you make friends with people of different ages and backgrounds. It's also a great way of socialising with your current friends.

2) By taking part in team activities like football, you have to practise teamwork — how to cooperate and work with other people. These skills are useful in all walks of life and can help you to be successful, which will increase your sense of worth. Being part of a team can help you to feel more involved in society as a whole.

3) For many people, physical activity probably won't put a roof over their heads. But the skills you learn through exercise and sport can help you succeed at work as well as at the gym or on the playing field.

*Rita made lots of new friends on the hockey field.*

---

### Pumping iron with a grin on your face — serotonin' up...

These benefits are less obvious than those on the last page — especially the social health ones. But take your time and jot them down again and again until you've got them all stored in your head. Then try this Practice Question...

Q1  Give **two** emotional health benefits of exercise. [2 marks]

Section Four — Health, Fitness and Well-being

# Lifestyle Choices

Lifestyle choices — like how you eat and drink, whether or not you smoke and how much sleep you get — will all have a knock-on effect on your fitness and your health. So, choose wisely and read this whole page.

## Key Lifestyle Choices — Think DRAW

There are four areas of lifestyle choices that you need to know — Diet, Recreational drugs, Activity level and your Work/rest/sleep balance. The first letters spell DRAW, which is handy for remembering them.

### 1) Diet

*Pages 40-42 cover diet in more depth...*

1) A balanced diet helps support a healthy lifestyle. Your body needs the right nutrients to work well — and these nutrients provide energy so you can exercise and improve your health.
2) A diet that's too high in some fats, sugar or salt can have negative effects on your health and can increase the risk of obesity. Too much salt can also increase blood pressure. This increases the risk of strokes and heart disease.
3) Not eating enough is also dangerous and can lead to malnutrition — this is where the body does not have enough nutrients to maintain good health.

### 2) Recreational Drugs — Alcohol and Nicotine

**ALCOHOL**

1) Alcohol affects your coordination, speech and judgement. Your reaction time gets slower.
2) Drinking large amounts often causes an increase in blood pressure, so increases your risk of stroke and heart disease.
3) Eventually, heavy drinking will damage your liver, heart, muscles, brain and the digestive and immune systems.

**SMOKING**

1) The chemicals in cigarette smoke cause damage to cells in the lungs and small hairs in your windpipe called cilia.
2) This increases the risk of getting infections, which can lead to bronchitis (inflammation of the major airways) or pneumonia (inflammation deep in the lungs).
3) The damage to alveoli causes them to lose their shape, so they work less efficiently. This is called emphysema.
4) The damage to your lungs can also cause lung cancer.
5) Tobacco also contains the addictive drug nicotine, which raises your heart rate and blood pressure.

*You know, your smoking really irritates me.*

*Any damage to the lungs makes breathing more difficult so affects fitness and performance.*

### 3) Activity Level

To be healthy, you need to be active. See p36-37 for all the positive effects of physical activity and how it can reduce health risks. There's more about the impact of an inactive lifestyle on the next page.

To improve health and fitness, you can design a personal exercise programme (PEP — see p25). Your PEP should be tailored to your individual needs and monitored so you get the benefits you want.

### 4) Work/Rest/Sleep Balance

1) You need to make time to rest and relax after work to help relieve any stress or anxiety you're feeling.
2) If you're feeling stressed, your blood pressure increases. If this continues over a long period of time, it increases the risk of heart disease and strokes.
3) Stress and anxiety also affect your emotional well-being. They can cause insomnia (trouble sleeping) and depression.
4) Sleep is vital for your body as it allows it to rest and recover after a day's work.
5) Lack of sleep affects your ability to concentrate. It also makes you uncoordinated and your muscles become fatigued quicker. In the long term it can lead to anxiety and depression.

## Jim's started smoking — that boy's getting cilia and cilia...

Some of the topics on this page are covered in more detail on other pages. Not the stuff about smoking, drinking and work/rest/sleep balance though, so make sure you learn that good and proper. Exam Practice Question time...

Q1  Explain **one** way that smoking can have a negative impact on health. [3 marks]

Section Four — Health, Fitness and Well-being

# Sedentary Lifestyle

Couch potatoes be warned — sitting around all day is not good for you. Apart from sitting around all day revising — that's very good for you, so get nice and comfy and 'ave a butcher's at this...

## A Sedentary Lifestyle has Many Long-term Health Risks

Basically, if you have a sedentary lifestyle, it means you don't exercise enough:

**A sedentary lifestyle is one where there is little, irregular or no physical activity.**

1) If you aren't active enough, you might not use up all the energy you get from food. Any excess energy is stored as fat. This increases your risk of becoming overweight, overfat or even obese.

| Being OVERWEIGHT means weighing more than is normal. | Being OVERFAT means having more body fat than you should. | Being OBESE means having a lot more body fat than you should. |

2) Being overfat (or obese) puts more strain on your cardiovascular system and decreases cardiovascular fitness. Increased body fat can also lead to fatty deposits in the arteries, making it harder for the heart to pump blood. This increases blood pressure and the risk of strokes and coronary heart disease.

3) You are also more likely to develop type-2 diabetes if you are obese (see p36).

4) A sedentary lifestyle also has negative effects on the musculo-skeletal system. Being overweight puts strain on your back and joints, which can lead to bad posture and joint damage. By not exercising enough the body loses muscle tone and is less good at repairing and strengthening bones, which increases the risk of osteoporosis.

5) Being overweight decreases flexibility, speed and agility, so affects your performance too.

6) A sedentary lifestyle can also lead to emotional health problems like depression.

## Data About Health Issues can be Plotted as a Graph

You can analyse data on health issues to understand how things are changing over time. This allows you to spot trends and make predictions about the future.

Here's an example of the kind of graph you could get in your exam, and the sort of things you'll need to say about it:

NB: You will not be allowed a crystal ball in the exam.

- You can either describe what's happening over time (see 1), or at certain points in time (see 2 and 3).
- Be specific — give the exact dates for the part of the graph you're describing — e.g. 'in 2010', 'from 1993 to 2009'.
- Make sure you say enough to get all the marks.
- If you're asked to describe or predict a trend from the graph, you need to look at the graph as a whole to see whether it is going up or going down in the long term. Then you need to predict whether this is likely to continue. E.g. in the graph above, there's a general upward trend in obesity rates for men and women. This trend looks like it will continue for men, but rates for women have started decreasing.

Percentage of obese adults (16+) in England from 1993 to 2013

① From 1993 to 2009, women had a higher obesity rate than men.
② In 2009 obesity rates for men and women were lower than they were in 2008.
③ In 2010, men had a higher obesity rate than women for the first time.

Source: Health Survey for England 2014. Health and Social Care Information Centre.

This trend is out of control...

### Sedentary? Not me — I get up and put the kettle on sometimes...

Data questions pop up everywhere — not just here — so make sure you really get to grips with what it means to 'analyse a graph' and 'predict a trend'. Then have a go at this Exam Practice Question...

Q1  Give **two** long-term health risks that are increased by a sedentary lifestyle. [2 marks]

Section Four — Health, Fitness and Well-being

# Diet and Nutrition

If you are what you eat, why didn't Popeye turn green? Anyway, a big part of being healthy is having a balanced diet. This means getting the right amount of nutrients to support your lifestyle. Mmm nutrients...

## You Should Eat a Balanced Diet to be Healthy

1) Eating a balanced diet is an important part of being healthy and helps you perform well in sport.
2) What makes up a balanced diet is slightly different for everyone. E.g. if you exercise loads, you'll need to eat more high-energy foods than someone who doesn't.

> A balanced diet contains the best ratio of nutrients to match your lifestyle.

*See p42 for how diet can be suited to different activities...*

3) The 'best ratio' means the right amount of each nutrient in relation to the other nutrients.
4) A balanced diet supports your lifestyle by providing the energy and the nutrients your body needs to work well. It helps to prevent health problems and injury, and to speed up recovery following exercise.

## You Need More of Some Nutrients Than Others

There are two main groups of nutrients your body needs:

Macronutrients — nutrients your body needs in large amounts.

Micronutrients — nutrients your body still needs, but in smaller amounts.

**MACRONUTRIENTS:**
Proteins    Fats    Carbohydrates

**MICRONUTRIENTS:**
Vitamins    Minerals

On top of these, you also need plenty of water and fibre in your diet (see next page). The best way to get all of these nutrients is to eat a varied diet with plenty of fruit and vegetables.

## Carbohydrates, Fats and Proteins Give You Energy

Carbohydrates, fats and proteins are macronutrients — they make up a lot of your food. They provide you with energy and help you grow and repair.

### CARBOHYDRATES

1) For most people, carbohydrates are the main source of energy for the body. Carbohydrates are vital for providing energy for your muscles during physical activity.
2) You can get simple ones like sugar, and complex ones, e.g. starch from pasta or rice.
3) Whenever you eat carbohydrates, some will get used by the body straight away.
4) The rest gets stored in the liver and muscles, ready for when it's needed (or turned into fat).

*Oh, I'm very complex y'know.*

### FATS

1) Fats are made from molecules called fatty acids.
2) They provide energy for low-intensity exercise. They also help to keep the body warm and protect organs, which helps to prevent injury.
3) Some vitamins can only be absorbed by the body using fats.
4) Fats are a source of the 'essential fatty acids' omega-3 and omega-6.

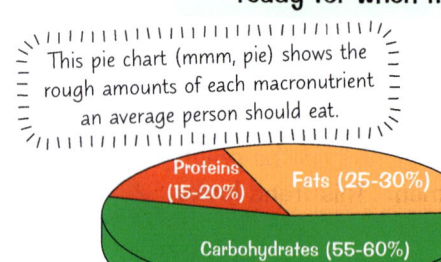

*This pie chart (mmm, pie) shows the rough amounts of each macronutrient an average person should eat.*

Proteins (15-20%)
Fats (25-30%)
Carbohydrates (55-60%)

### PROTEINS

1) Proteins help the body grow and repair itself. They're vital for building and repairing muscles after exercise.
2) They're made from molecules called amino acids — your body can make new proteins from the amino acids you get from food.
3) Meat, fish, eggs and beans are all rich in protein.

---

### A balanced diet — dead important for tight-rope walkers...

Make sure that you understand how carbohydrates, proteins and fats help you to do physical activity.

Q1   Which macronutrient should you eat most of in a balanced diet?                    [1 mark]

Section Four — Health, Fitness and Well-being

# Diet and Nutrition

Micronutrients are just as important as macronutrients — you just need smaller amounts of them.

## You need Small Amounts of Vitamins and Minerals

**VITAMINS**

1) Vitamins help your bones, teeth, skin and other tissues to grow. They're also needed for many of the body's chemical reactions, e.g. some are used in the processes that release energy from food.
2) Fat-soluble vitamins can be stored in the body. Here are a couple of examples:
   - Vitamin A — needed for your growth and vision. It can be found in meat, fish and eggs.
   - Vitamin D — needed for strong bones so helps to prevent injury and osteoporosis. It can be made by the skin in sunshine, but it's also found in milk, fish, liver and eggs.
3) Water-soluble vitamins can't be stored, so you need to eat them regularly. For example:
   - Vitamin C — good for your skin and helps to hold your body tissues together. It's also really important for your immune system, so helps you to stay healthy so you can train and perform well. It's found in fruit and veg — especially in lemons, oranges and other citrus fruit.

**MINERALS**

1) Needed for healthy bones and teeth, and to build other tissues.
2) Minerals help in various chemical reactions in the body:
   - Calcium — needed for strong bones and teeth, but also for muscle contraction. Lots in green vegetables, milk and cheese.
   - Iron — used in making red blood cells, which carry oxygen round the body, e.g. to the muscles. There's tons in beans and green vegetables.

*Earl     Mini-earl*

## Water and Fibre are Just as Important

**WATER**

1) Water is needed in loads of chemical reactions in the body. It's also used in sweat to help you cool down when your body temperature rises, e.g. through exercise. As well as sweating, you also lose water through your breath, urine and faeces.
2) If you don't drink enough to replace the water you've used or lost, you become dehydrated. This can cause:
   - Blood thickening — you guessed it, the blood gets thicker. This makes it harder for the heart to pump the blood around and decreases the flow of oxygen to the muscles, so you can't perform as well.
   - An increase in body temperature, which could lead to overheating and maybe even fainting through heat exhaustion.
3) Rehydration with water or sports drinks during and after physical activity helps avoid dehydration. This is important in endurance events and hot climates where you sweat more.
4) Sports drinks have sugar in them to replace the energy your muscles have used up. They also contain a bit of salt which helps the water rehydrate you quickly.

**FIBRE**

1) You need fibre to keep your digestive system working properly. Good digestion means that your body gets all the nutrients it needs from food, so you're healthy and can do physical activity.
2) There's lots of fibre in fruit and vegetables — another good reason to eat loads of them.

*Not the best way to increase your fibre intake.*

---

### Ask your teacher if fibre is important for fartlek training...

... But don't blame me if you get into trouble. Time for a little Exam Practice Question? I think so...

Q1 Explain how exercise can cause dehydration. [2 marks]

*Section Four — Health, Fitness and Well-being*

# Diet, Nutrition and Performance

Eating for sport ain't all hot-dog guzzling contests and chilli cook-offs... You need to know how your diet can affect your performance and how different activities need different nutrients at different times.

## Different Types of Physical Activity Require Different Nutrients

1) The type of physical activity you are doing affects the balance of nutrients you need.
2) If your activity involves long periods of continuous exercise, like competing in a triathlon, you need a diet rich in carbohydrates. This is because carbohydrates provide plenty of energy that is easily available for your muscles. Fat is also an important energy source for endurance athletes as it can provide energy for low to moderate intensity exercise when supplies of carbohydrates are running low. 
3) If your activity involves gaining muscle bulk — like sprinting or weightlifting, you need a diet rich in protein in order to build and repair your muscles.
4) Carrying around extra weight as fat can affect performance. So, for many physical activities, you will want a diet that helps keep body fat low.
5) Hydration (the body having the right amount of water) is really important when you're exercising (see p41). It's especially important to take in water during activities where you sweat a lot and have an increased breathing rate for a long period of time.

## Organise Your Meals Around Activities

It's not just what you eat — when you eat is really important too if you want to perform well.
1) You should drink to replace lost fluid both during and after an activity (see p41).
2) You shouldn't eat during exercise, or for a couple of hours before, due to blood shunting:

> When you exercise, blood is redistributed around the body to increase the supply of oxygen to your muscles (see p7).
> This means blood is taken away from your digestive system — which makes it harder for you to digest food, so you end up feeling sick.

3) After exercise, within an hour, you should start eating to replace used energy.

## Endurance Athletes use Carbohydrate Loading Before Events

1) Endurance athletes will often increase their carbohydrate intake a few days before an event.
2) They'll also take it easy in training just before the event, so that most of those carbohydrates are not used up.
3) This increases the amount of energy the athlete has stored in their muscles, giving them plenty of energy for the event.

## Timing Protein Intake Helps Muscle Growth

1) The body isn't as good at storing protein as it is at storing some other nutrients. This means power athletes, like weightlifters and body-builders, will eat protein regularly so it's available for muscle growth and repair.
2) They might also take in protein at certain times to maximise their muscle growth. E.g. within an hour of doing a workout — when the muscles need to recover and repair themselves, so need protein to rebuild.
3) Also, your body repairs itself while you sleep, so power athletes will make sure they get plenty of protein before bed.

*Warning: cheese before bed may cause nightmares...*

## I preferred the sequel — 'Carbo-reloaded: revenge of the spuds'...

That's the end of the diet pages. Make sure you know who benefits from carbohydrate loading and timing protein intake, and why. Once you've got it, do this Exam Practice Question and make yourself a celebratory sandwich...

Q1  Justify whether a weightlifter or a triathlete would benefit more from carbohydrate loading.  [3 marks]

Section Four — Health, Fitness and Well-being

# Optimum Weight

This page is all about weight and how it's connected to performance. You need to know all the factors affecting your optimum weight and also how to maintain a healthy weight through your energy balance...

## Optimum Weight Depends on Different Things...

Your optimum weight is roughly what you should weigh for good health, based on these four factors that differ from person to person:

1) **HEIGHT** — The taller someone is, the larger their body, so the higher their optimum weight.
2) **BONE STRUCTURE** — some people have a larger or more dense bone structure than others. This means their skeleton will be heavier, so their optimum weight will be higher.
3) **MUSCLE GIRTH** — this is a measurement of the circumference of (the distance around) your muscles when they're flexed. Some people naturally have more muscle than others — they'll have a larger muscle girth and a higher optimum weight.
4) **GENDER** — men and women naturally have different body compositions. Men usually have larger bone structures and more muscle than women, so men generally have higher optimum weights.

## Optimum Weight will Vary for Different Sports...

A sportsperson's optimum weight is the weight at which they perform best. Optimum weight will vary depending on the activity or sport — e.g. a sumo wrestler will want to be heavier than a mountain climber.

1) Some sports require competitors to be within a certain weight class — e.g. a boxer's optimum fighting weight needs to be within their weight division.
2) In sports like rugby or American football, players have a large amount of muscle mass because they need strength and power. This means their optimum weight will be higher.
3) Similarly, some sports require performers to be light — e.g. a gymnast needs to hold their own body weight, so being light is an advantage.
4) Endurance athletes will want to be lighter than sprinters as they have to carry their weight for longer. Sprinters need large amounts of muscle to generate power, so have a higher optimum weight.

## Your Energy Balance controls your Weight

How much energy you need from food depends on how much you use up through bodily processes (things like breathing and digestion), daily activities and exercise.
Your energy balance is the relationship between the energy you take in and the energy you use:

1) If you take in more energy than you use, you have a positive energy balance. Spare energy is stored as fat, which causes you to gain weight.
2) If you don't take in enough food to match the energy you need, you have a negative energy balance. Your body makes up the difference by using up the energy stored in body fat. This causes you to lose weight.
3) If you want to maintain a healthy weight, you need to make sure you balance your energy intake with the energy you use up. This is called a neutral energy balance.

### How many star jumps 'til I can have the cake?

There's a ton of things on this page you need to know. You could say this page is heavy with facts. It's certainly not lightweight. So, make sure you learn it all and tip those scales in your favour for the exam...

Q1 Give **two** reasons why two women of the same height could have different optimum weights. [2 marks]

Section Four — Health, Fitness and Well-being

# Revision Questions for Section Four

That's it for Section Four. Give yourself a little time to digest all that information (ho ho ho), then fingers on buzzers for the Section Four revision questions...
- Try these questions and tick off each one when you get it right.
- When you've done all the questions for a topic and are completely happy with it, tick off the topic.
- The answers can all be found by looking back over pages 36 to 43.

## Health, Fitness and Well-being (p36-37) ☐

1) Give two physical health benefits of physical activity.
2) What effect does regular aerobic exercise have on blood pressure?
3) Which bone disease can weight-bearing exercise help prevent?
4) How can exercise make you feel good?
5) Give two social health benefits of sport.
6) Physical activity can increase your confidence. Is this a physical, emotional or social benefit?

## Lifestyle Choices and a Sedentary Lifestyle (p38-39) ☐

7) How can diet have a positive effect on health?
8) What effect does alcohol have on blood pressure?
9) State two health problems that can be caused by smoking.
10) Give one long-term effect of not getting enough sleep.
11) Define a 'sedentary lifestyle'. How is it connected to obesity?
12) What are two health risks associated with a sedentary lifestyle?

## Diet, Nutrition and Optimum Weight (p40-43) ☐

13) What is a 'balanced diet'?
14) Are proteins macronutrients or micronutrients? How about vitamins?
15) Name a macronutrient that provides lots of energy that can easily be used by the body.
16) How does protein help you recover after exercise?
17) Give two reasons why the body needs vitamins.
18) Which mineral is necessary for making red blood cells?
19) Explain what happens to your blood when you become dehydrated.
20) What role does fibre play in a balanced diet?
21) What type of athlete uses carbohydrate loading?
22) Why might a sprinter have a diet high in protein?
23) Give three factors that affect optimum weight.
24) If you take in more energy from food than you use up, do you lose weight?
25) How can an athlete maintain a healthy weight?

Section Four — Health, Fitness and Well-being

# Section Five — Sport Psychology

# Skills and Practice

This page is all about the different types of skill and practice, and about being mentally ready for performance.

## There are Different Types of Skill

1) Skill is a word we use all the time. Here's what it means in PE:

> A SKILL is a learned ability to bring about the result you want, with confidence and minimum effort.

2) You need to know about three ways to classify skills:

### OPEN VS CLOSED SKILLS

1) An open skill is performed in a changing environment, where a performer has to react and adapt to external factors. E.g. during a football tackle, you need to adapt to things such as the position of other players on the pitch.
2) A closed skill is always performed in the same predictable environment — it's not affected by external factors. E.g. when breaking off in snooker, the conditions are the same every time.

### LOW VS HIGH ORGANISATION SKILLS

1) A low organisation skill is one which can easily be broken down into different parts that can be practised separately. E.g. the front crawl stroke in swimming.
2) A high organisation skill is one which can't easily be broken down into different parts that can be practised separately, because the parts of the skill are closely linked. E.g. a cartwheel.

### BASIC VS COMPLEX SKILLS

1) A basic skill (or 'simple' skill) is one which doesn't need much concentration to do, e.g. running.
2) A complex skill is one which needs lots of concentration to do, e.g. a volley in football.

3) Most skills come somewhere in between these classifications. You can show this by putting skills on a 'continuum' (or 'scale') with one category on each end.
4) For example, you can compare the "openness" of skills by putting them on a scale like this one:
5) You can also put skills on a scale from basic to complex, or from low to high organisation.

CLOSED — Skipping, Throwing a dart, High jump, Catching a cricket ball, Football tackle — OPEN

## You need Practice to Improve a Skill

*The breaks can also be used to get feedback on a skill (see p47).*

There are four different types of practice you need to know about:

**MASSED** — This means practising the skill continuously without a break. It works well to improve basic skills.

**DISTRIBUTED** — This means practising with breaks for rest or mental rehearsal (see below). It works well to improve complex skills — you might need a break because the skill is difficult.

**FIXED** — This means repeating the same technique in one situation over and over again. This makes it useful for practising closed skills. It is sometimes known as doing 'drills'.

**VARIABLE** — This means repeating the technique in different situations that you might need to use it in. It's useful for practising open skills.

## You can Mentally Prepare for Sport

1) Being mentally prepared is all about being able to get in the 'zone'. It can help you keep control of your emotions and cope with stress so you can perform at your best.
2) One way to mentally prepare is mental rehearsal — imagining yourself performing well.
3) Practising your skills during a warm-up can also help you mentally prepare (see p31).
4) All this can help you focus on what you need to do and raise your confidence.

---

### Mentally rehearse your exam for guaranteed success...

Lots of definitions on this page, so make sure you know them all for the exam. Have a go at this Practice Question.

Q1  Explain why a gymnast might use distributed practice to improve a dismount.  [3 marks]

# Goal Setting

Setting goals and targets can often seem a bit of a hassle. But if you put the effort in and set them properly, not only do you have something to aim for, but reaching your targets can make you feel ace.

## Goal Setting can Help you Train

1) Goal setting means setting targets that you want to reach so you can improve your performance.
2) Short-term goals that you can reach quite quickly are steps on the way to a long-term one — like winning an Olympic medal.

Goal setting helps training because:
1) It gives you something to aim for and motivates you to work hard.
2) Reaching a goal can boost your confidence and can give you a sense of achievement.

Geoff's Goals:
Long term — become an Olympic diver
Short term — get over his fear of heights

## Goal Setting Should be SMART

When you're setting targets make sure they're SMART.

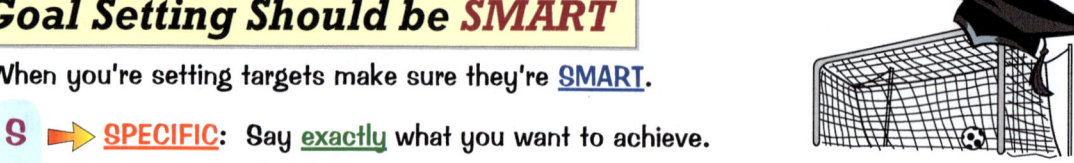

**S → SPECIFIC**: Say exactly what you want to achieve.
1) You need to have a specific target and outline exactly what you need to do to achieve it.
2) This makes sure you're focused on your goal.
3) E.g. 'My goal is to swim 1000 m continuously'.

**M → MEASURABLE**: Goals need to be measurable.
1) This is so you can see how much you've progressed towards your goal over time — so you stay motivated to train.
2) E.g. 'My goal is to run 100 m in under 12 seconds'.

**A → ACHIEVABLE**: You need to make sure your targets are set at the right level of difficulty. If a target's too easy, it won't motivate you. If it's too difficult, you might start to feel negative about your performance, and give up.

**R → REALISTIC**: Set targets you can realistically reach.
1) This means making sure you have everything you need to be able to fulfil your target.
2) That could mean being physically able to do something, or having enough resources (time, money, facilities...) to be able to reach your target.
3) This is so you stay determined during training — if it's not realistic, you could be put off.

**T → TIME-BOUND**: Set a deadline for reaching your goal.
1) You need a time limit to make sure your target is measurable.
2) Meeting short-term target deadlines keeps you on course to reach your long-term goals in time.
3) This keeps you motivated — you'll want to train to achieve your goal in time for your deadline.

As well as setting targets, you need to make sure you review them regularly. This is so you can see how much you've progressed towards your goal and what else you need to do to achieve it.

## Goal setting — jumpers for goal posts...

Make sure you know what SMART stands for and how it can improve performance. Now try a Practice Question...

Q1  An athlete sets herself a goal to increase her running speed in six weeks.
    State **one** principle of SMART goal setting that this goal does not apply. Explain your answer. [2 marks]

Section Five — Sport Psychology

# Guidance and Feedback

To learn or improve a skill, you might need some guidance and feedback to help you.

## Guidance — How to Perform or Develop a Skill

There are lots of different types of guidance a coach or trainer can give:

1) **VERBAL** — An explanation in words of how to perform a technique.

   *Have a look at p45 for definitions of the different skill types.*

   **ADVANTAGES**
   1) Can be combined with other types of guidance.
   2) Helpful for experienced performers who'll understand any technical language.
   3) Can give guidance during a performance. This is especially useful for improving open skills.

   **DISADVANTAGES**
   1) Less useful for teaching high organisation and complex skills which are difficult to explain.
   2) Could be confusing for a beginner if it uses complicated language.

2) **VISUAL** — Visual clues to help you perform a technique. A coach could use demonstrations or videos and diagrams of a technique to show how it should be performed.

   **ADVANTAGES**
   1) Works well for beginners — they can copy the skill.
   2) Can be used to teach low organisation skills — each part of the skill can be shown step by step.

   **DISADVANTAGES**
   Less useful for teaching complex and high organisation skills — they're more complicated and difficult to copy.

3) **MANUAL** — When the coach physically moves your body through the technique. For example, a coach might guide your arms when you're practising a golf swing.

   **ADVANTAGES**
   1) You can get the "feel" of a skill before doing it on your own.
   2) Works well to teach people of all skill levels.

   *Learning by doing an action is known as kinaesthetic learning.*

   **DISADVANTAGES**
   1) A performer could start to rely on it and not able to perform a skill without it.
   2) Difficult to use with big groups of learners.

4) **MECHANICAL** — Guidance given using sport equipment, e.g. a harness in trampolining.

   **ADVANTAGES**
   1) Useful for teaching beginners — they can feel safe while practising a new skill that might normally be dangerous, e.g. a somersault.
   2) Helpful for teaching complex and high organisation skills.

   **DISADVANTAGES**
   1) A learner might be unable to perform the skill without the help of the equipment.
   2) Difficult to use in large groups.

## Feedback — Finding Out How You Did

*For an example of interpreting data showing how someone performed, see page 55.*

1) Feedback can be either intrinsic or extrinsic:

   **INTRINSIC** — you know how well you did the technique because of what it 'felt' like. This works best for experienced performers — they can judge whether or not they've performed well.
   **EXTRINSIC** — someone else tells you or shows you what happened, and how to improve. This is suited to beginners — they don't have the experience or knowledge to accurately assess their own performance.

2) These types of feedback can be either concurrent or terminal:

   **CONCURRENT FEEDBACK** is received during a performance.
   **TERMINAL FEEDBACK** is received after a performance.

3) You can use feedback to work out your strengths and weaknesses and come up with an action plan to improve your performance.

---

### Verbal guidance is just what it sounds like...

Make sure you know the advantages and disadvantages of these guidance types. You need to be able to decide whether a certain type is suitable for teaching a particular group a skill. Here's an Exam Practice Question to try...

Q1  Evaluate the use of verbal and manual guidance to improve a beginner's performance in golf.  [9 marks]

*Section Five — Sport Psychology*

# Revision Questions for Section Five

Section Five has come to an end, so let's see how much you've learned.
- Try these questions and tick off each one when you get it right.
- When you've done all the questions for a topic and are completely happy with it, tick off the topic.
- The answers can all be found by looking back over pages 45 to 47.

## Skills and Practice (p45) ☐

1) What is the difference between an open and a closed skill?
2) Which type of skill can be broken down into separate parts?
3) Which type of skill needs lots of concentration to perform?
4) Give two examples of an open skill.
5) What is the difference between massed and distributed practice?
6) Explain the difference between fixed and variable practice.
7) What is meant by 'mental preparation'? Why does it help to be mentally prepared for an activity?
8) How might an athlete mentally prepare for a performance?

## Goal Setting (p46) ☐

9) Why might a performer set themselves a goal?
10) What do the letters in SMART stand for? Choose from:
    A  Specific, measurable, achievable, realistic, time-bound
    B  Sensible, measurable, actual, realistic, timed
    C  Sensible, measurable, achievable, realistic, time-bound
    D  Specific, meaningful, achievable, realistic, timed
11) Explain the meaning and benefits of each element of SMART.
12) Why should you review your targets and goals regularly?

## Guidance and Feedback (p47) ☐

13) What is guidance?
14) What is verbal guidance and why is it more suited to more experienced performers?
15) What is visual guidance? Why is it effective for teaching low organisation skills?
    Why is it less effective for teaching high organisation skills?
16) Give an example of manual guidance.
17) What is mechanical guidance?
18) What disadvantage do manual and mechanical guidance have in common?
19) What is feedback?
20) Explain the difference between intrinsic and extrinsic feedback.
21) Explain what is meant by:
    a) Concurrent feedback
    b) Terminal feedback

# Section Six — Sport, Society and Culture

# Influences on Participation

Participation rates are how many people take part in sport or other physical activities. Whether you participate in sports, and the type of sports you play, can be affected by lots of different factors...

## Your *Gender* may *Influence* whether you do *Activity*

Although things are getting better, there's still a real gender divide in participation. Surveys carried out by Sport England show that, overall, fewer women participate regularly in sport than men.

1) This may be because many women's events have a lower profile then men's, as they get less media coverage. This has meant that in many sports there are fewer female role models to inspire younger generations to take up the sport.

2) Less media coverage also means there is less sponsorship available for women's sport, meaning there are fewer opportunities and less money for women to do sport at a higher level.

*In football, the team who won the 2015 women's world cup got $2 million. The 2014 men's winner got $35 million. Hmmm...*

3) Gender may also affect what sports you decide to take up — outdated and stupid attitudes about some things being "women's activities" and others being "men's activities" still exist.

## *Ethnicity* can have an *Effect* too

1) Sometimes your religious beliefs or ethnic background can influence the physical activity you do.

> E.g. many Muslim women keep their bodies covered up. This may mean they're less likely to participate in activities such as swimming because of the clothing that's expected to be worn.

2) The culture you grow up in will also have an effect on what sports you participate in — if your friends or your family play a particular sport, you'll be more likely to play that sport too.

3) Racism and racial abuse used to be a huge problem in sport. Campaigns against racism, such as the Let's Kick Racism Out Of Football campaign, have helped bring the problem of racism into the media. Unfortunately, incidents of racial abuse still do happen, e.g. racist chanting at football matches.

## Your *Socio-Economic Group* can also have an *Effect*

Socio-economic groups are just a fancy way of grouping people based on how much money they have, where they live and the type of job they do.

- "Working class", "middle class" and "young professional" are all examples of socio-economic groups.

*Yaaaar, I'm a Yuppie — a Young, Upwardly-mobile Pirate.*

Recent studies seem to show that, in general, people in lower socio-economic groups are less likely to regularly take part in sport. Also, the kinds of activities people do can be affected by their socio-economic group.

1) Most sports cost money. This means that some people can't afford to take part.

2) Lots of sports — like horse riding, skiing, sailing and even cycling — require specialist equipment and clothing. This can be very expensive, so could prevent people from taking part.

3) Some sports require special facilities — like ski slopes or ice rinks. If you don't live in an area with these sorts of facilities, you won't easily be able to do those sports.

4) If you don't have access to a car or good public transport to get to the facilities, this makes it a lot harder to participate. You'll be more likely to do a more accessible sport like football or basketball.

5) If you work shifts or irregular hours it can be hard to join clubs or groups that meet in the evenings or at the weekend.

---

### We're all under the influence...

You need to understand how all these personal factors can have an effect on participation rates and what sports people participate in. And now, treat yourself and have a pop at this Exam Practice Question...

Q1 State two reasons why your socio-economic group could affect whether you play sport. [2 marks]

Section Six — Sport, Society and Culture

# Influences on Participation

Another page of influences on participation, I'm afraid. Don't worry though — it's the last one. Age and disability might also affect whether you play sport and the kind of activities you do...

## Age can Limit the Activities you can do

1) Some sports are more popular than others with different age groups.
2) Most people aged 16-30 have loads of choice for physical activity.
3) People over 50 are more physically limited in the sports they can choose. They tend to do less strenuous activities like walking or swimming.
4) Some sports, such as weightlifting or endurance events, can potentially damage a young person's body. Competitions in these sorts of activities often have a minimum age restriction.
5) Young people often have more spare time to do sport. As people get older and have careers and families, there's less time available for playing sport.

## Disability will Influence you too...

1) Having a disability can limit the physical activities you can do. Studies show that participation rates for disabled people are lower than they are for non-disabled people.
2) The opportunities in sport and access to sporting facilities for disabled people used to be few and far between.
3) Nowadays, there are many schemes set up to give disabled people more opportunity to exercise and take part in activities within their physical limits.
4) Disabled sporting events are now given a lot more media coverage than they once were. The Paralympics now gets extensive media coverage, like the Olympics.
5) This media coverage is helping to change people's attitudes towards disability and sport.
6) It's also helping create many more disabled role models (like Dame Tanni Grey-Thompson and Ellie Simmonds), which encourages more disabled people to get active.

## You'll Need to Interpret Data about Participation Rates

In the exam, you'll need to be able to analyse graphs showing participation rates for different sports and activities.

1) You may get asked to compare activities, e.g. to say which activity has increased or decreased most from one point to another.
2) The bigger the difference between these two points, the bigger the increase or decrease.
3) For example, the graph on the right shows that:
   - Participation in running increased more than football or cycling from 07/08 to 10/11.
   - Participation in football decreased more than cycling or running from 11/12 to 12/13.

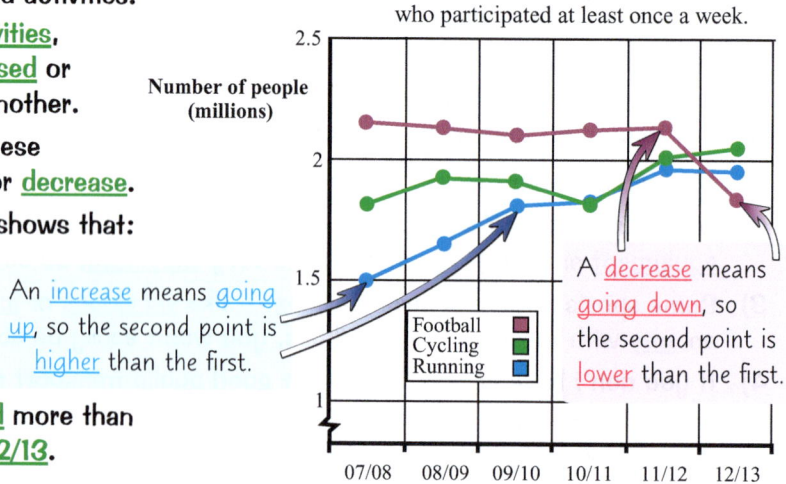

An increase means going up, so the second point is higher than the first.

A decrease means going down, so the second point is lower than the first.

Graph showing the number of English people aged 16 or over who participated at least once a week.

---

## Participation — you've got to be in it to win it...

You could get a graph showing participation rates for different groups — e.g. rates for men and women. You might need to use the reasons covered on these pages to explain the differences too. Now, Practice Question time.

Q1  Using the graph above, which of these sports had the highest participation rate in 2012-13?
   A Football        B Cycling        C Running        D Golf        [1 mark]

Section Six — Sport, Society and Culture

# Commercialisation of Sport

You can't get away from sport — it's in the news, on the TV and all over social media. And all those teams and sportspeople are sponsored by companies. This is the commercialisation of sport. Here are the facts...

## Commercialisation Means Making Money

1) There's a lot of money around in some sports, because they've become commercialised.
2) The commercialisation of sport is all about making money from it.
3) A lot of money comes from sponsorship — if people are going to see it, companies will slap their name on it, whether it's a person, team, league, stand, trophy, mascot, badge or ball. This is great advertising for the sponsor.
4) Money also comes from the media. The lion's share of this is from television companies, but radio and newspapers still play a part.
5) The media pay so they can cover the sport, which means people will buy their newspaper or watch their TV show. Some companies sell sport on TV, or over the Internet, as a subscription package too.
6) Sports also make money through selling tickets to events, and merchandise.

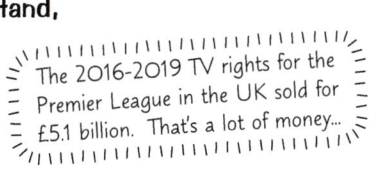

*The 2016-2019 TV rights for the Premier League in the UK sold for £5.1 billion. That's a lot of money...*

## Sport, the Media and Commercialisation are all Connected

Sport, the media and sponsorship have grown to depend on one another. There are advantages and disadvantages to this relationship for the sponsor, the sport, the players and the spectators.

### SPONSORSHIP AND SPORT

1) Sponsorship deals mean companies can associate their name with the prestige of successful sportspeople and teams. This is a very effective form of advertising, which helps the sponsor to make more money.
2) These deals mean big money for sport — which can be spent on development, e.g. of a new stadium or facilities. This benefits the players and the spectators.
3) Sponsorship money also means players can be paid good wages, and they can train full-time. This benefits everyone, because they will perform better.
4) Sometimes, the money is only available for the top players and teams, so only benefits the elite — not the sport as a whole.

### SPONSORSHIP AND THE MEDIA

1) The more media coverage a sport gets, the more people watch it. This makes sponsorship more valuable, as it can reach a larger audience.
2) This increases the likelihood of sponsorship and means the sport and players can demand more money for their sponsorship deals.

### THE MEDIA AND SPORT

1) The media pay for the rights to cover sporting events, which provides investment for sports to develop at lower levels.
2) Media coverage makes more people aware of the sport, so more people may play it.
3) Media coverage of elite players and athletes can create role models who inspire people to play.
4) This can make players into superstars. But, the downside is that players are hounded by the media and their private lives are all over the news.
5) Also, the media can hold so much power over sport that they'll change things:
   - The number of games played, or the timings of matches, might be changed so more matches can be shown. This risks injury to players through lack of rest, and might mean spectators miss a game because it's not at a convenient time.
   - Sometimes rules may be changed — e.g. in tennis, the tiebreaker set was brought in to make matches shorter.
6) More fans watching on TV or the Internet can mean fewer fans buying tickets. This means losses in ticket sales for the sport and a poorer atmosphere at the stadium for spectators.

### I don't write these jokes for the money — I do it for the love, man....

Well, actually no one will sponsor me. Apparently, lame puns and gags about fartlek training aren't the 'in thing'... Get this commercialisation stuff memorised and the marks will flow like famous footballers' sponsorship deals.

Q1 Explain **two** ways that media interest in a sport can encourage more people to take part. [4 marks]

Section Six — Sport, Society and Culture

# Commercialisation of Sport

Sponsorship can be a little complicated. You need to know that it has its downsides and that not all types of sponsor are suitable. Read on to find out about the dark side...

## Sponsorship Isn't All Great

1) It could all turn nasty — get injured, lose your form or get a bad reputation and it's bye-bye sponsorship deal.
2) Sometimes athletes have to fulfil contracts with their sponsor — they might have to turn up at a special event or appear in a TV advert (even if they don't want to).
3) Athletes can get into trouble with their sponsor if they're photographed using another company's products.
4) If a team really needs a sponsor's money, this puts the sponsor in a position of power. This means they can influence the team's playing style or team selection.

*Why's he playing?*
*His dad sponsors the team.*

## Some Sponsors are Inappropriate

Sponsorship brings in loads of money, but you have to be careful not to promote the wrong image, especially in youth sports:

1) Cigarette and tobacco companies aren't allowed to sponsor sports in the UK. This is because their products are harmful and unhealthy.
2) Alcoholic drinks companies are allowed to sponsor some sports, but this can be bad as it gives alcohol a false image of health. The same is true for unhealthy food companies.
3) Also, as sport is watched by children, advertising alcohol and fast food could be encouraging young people to drink or eat unhealthily.

## You'll Need to Interpret Data About Commercialisation

It's another one of those fun data bits. In your exam you could be asked to interpret data about the commercialisation of sport.

1) For example, the graph on the right shows the total amount spent each year on shirt sponsorship (that's companies paying to have their logo on the front of a team's shirt) in the Premier League.
2) The graph shows that every year since 2010, spending on shirt sponsorship in the Premier League has increased.
3) So there's an upward trend in spending on shirt sponsorship — and if the graph carried on past 2015, you'd expect it to keep on going upwards.
4) You can also see that the biggest increases in spending were from 2011 to 2012 and from 2014 to 2015 — shown by the line going up more steeply.

A graph showing the amount spent on shirt sponsorship in the Premier League between 2010 and 2015.

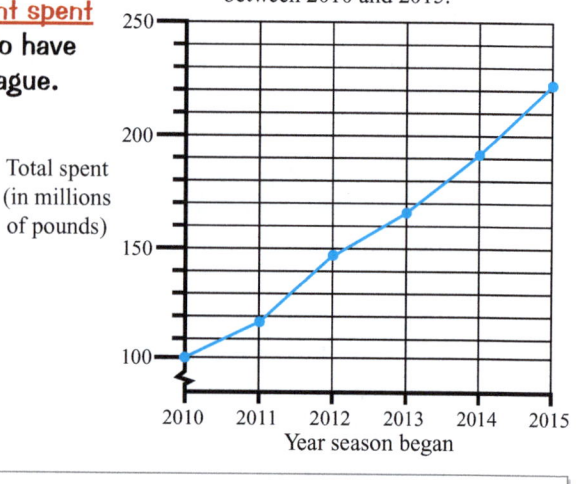

### CGP CGP CGP CGP (CGP — Official Sponsors of page 52)...

It's important that you can weigh up the pros and cons of sponsorship, especially when it comes to fast-food and alcohol companies. Have a go at this Exam Practice Question to check you've got it...

Q1 Assess the positive and negative impact on an under-12's football team of being sponsored by a fast-food company. [6 marks]

Section Six — Sport, Society and Culture

# Sporting Behaviour

Right, nearly there. Just this page about good and bad behaviour in sport to go. Sportsmanship is about good behaviour, whereas gamesmanship and deviance are both examples of bad behaviour in sport.

## Sportsmanship is About Being Fair and Humble

Being a good sportsperson is more than just playing by the rules. You also have to uphold the spirit of the game and treat your opponents with dignity and fairness. Even if you lose...

> Sportsmanship means being honest, sticking to the rules and treating your opponents with respect.

1) This means no rubbing it in the opposition's face if you win. And no going off in a huff if you lose.
2) It also means following unwritten rules, even if that means losing out when you don't need to, e.g.:
   - In cycling, if someone has a mechanical problem with their bike (like a puncture), the other riders will not take advantage by speeding up until the problem is fixed.
   - In cricket, a batsman might choose to 'walk' if they think they've been caught out — even if the umpire has ruled them not out.
   - In football, players will kick the ball out of play if a member of the other team goes down injured.

## Gamesmanship and Deviance — Types of Poor Behaviour

> Gamesmanship is gaining an advantage by using tactics that seem unfair, but aren't against the rules.

Gamesmanship is not actually cheating — but it can come quite close. A lot of the techniques are about breaking up the flow of a game, or distracting your opponents:

1) Time-wasting in football is when players deliberately faff about. This runs down the clock and breaks up the flow of the game.
2) In tennis, some players make loud grunting or shrieking noises when they hit the ball to try and intimidate or distract their opponent.
3) In basketball, a manager might call a timeout just as the opposition win a free throw. This is to try and make them overthink the shot.

Gamesmanship does not normally result in punishment for the players, although if it is taken too far referees might get involved.

> Deviance is behaviour that goes against the moral values or laws of the sport.

Deviance is breaking the rules. Sometimes it involves cheating to gain an advantage in the game:

1) Using performance-enhancing drugs or blood doping are both deviance because they give you an unfair advantage.
2) 'Professional fouls', like tripping someone to get ahead of them, are also deviance.

Other times it's being far too aggressive:

3) Cuban taekwondo athlete Angel Matos was banned from the sport for life after deliberately kicking a referee.
4) Boxer Mike Tyson and footballer Luis Suarez have both been in trouble for biting their opposition.

Deviance is punished by sports officials to discourage players from doing it:

1) For really serious offences, like using performance-enhancing drugs or biting, players may be banned from competing. There could also be a hefty fine.
2) For deviance like fouling an opponent, the referee or umpire may punish players by removing them from the field of play either temporarily — the 'sin bin', or permanently — a red card or disqualification.

Most forms of deviance happen more at the higher levels of a sport because there is so much at stake.

*See p57 for an example of data about ethical issues in sport...*

---

### Footballers ought to be gracious in defeat — they use 'em enough...

I know, it's easy to get confused between sportsmanship and gamesmanship. Just remember that sportsmanship is about 'being a good sport'. Now, one last Exam Practice Question to round off the section...

Q1  Describe the difference between deviance and gamesmanship.  [2 marks]

Section Six — Sport, Society and Culture

# Revision Questions for Section Six

That's Section Six done and dusted — now be a good sport and have a go at these revision questions.
Try these questions and tick off each one when you get it right.
- When you've done all the questions for a topic and are completely happy with it, tick off the topic.
- The answers can all be found by looking back over pages 49 to 53.

## Influences on Participation (p49-50)

1) Give two personal factors that could affect participation rates in sport.
2) How can your gender influence what sports you participate in?
3) What is meant by a socio-economic group?
4) Outline one way that the amount of money you have could affect your participation in sport.
5) Describe two ways that your age can limit your participation in physical activities.
6) Give one example of a sporting activity that is inappropriate for a very young person to participate in.
7) How can the media help improve participation rates amongst the disabled?
8) How do you spot an increase in a participation rate on a line graph?

## Commercialisation of Sport (p51-52)

9) What does 'commercialisation' mean?
10) Give one effect of increased media coverage on a sport.
11) Give one advantage and one disadvantage of sponsorship for a sport.
12) If a sports team gets media coverage, what might happen to the value of their sponsorship deals? Give a possible reason for this happening.
13) How can increased media coverage increase participation in a sport?
14) Why do companies sponsor sports?
15) Give one way an athlete could lose their sponsorship deal.
16) Which of these cannot sponsor a UK football team: a) a car manufacturer, b) a tobacco company?
17) Give an advantage and a disadvantage of a brewery sponsoring a youth games tournament.

## Sporting Behaviour (p53)

18) Give a definition and an example of:
    a) Sportsmanship
    b) Gamesmanship
    c) Deviance
19) Is time-wasting in football an example of gamesmanship or deviance? What about a 'professional foul'?
20) Name one possible punishment an athlete could face if they're caught blood-doping.
21) Is deviance more likely or less likely to happen in the higher levels of sport? Why?

# Using Data

You've got to be comfortable with interpreting data displayed in graphs and tables. Luckily for you, these three pages will go through how you do it. And you thought you could get away from maths by taking PE...

## There Are Two Different Types of Data

You can collect two different types of data — qualitative data and quantitative data:

*The easiest way to remember the difference is 'quantitative' sounds like 'quantity' — which means 'number of'...*

**Qualitative data describes something — it will be in words.**

1) Qualitative data can be collected through observation — e.g. 'the team played well', 'the athlete is strong' or 'the weather was cold'.
2) Or you can interview people. E.g. asking an athlete how they're feeling before a race might give you answers like "confident" or "well-prepared".
3) It's less easy to analyse than data in numbers.

**Quantitative data measures something — it will be in numbers.**

1) Quantitative data measures things — e.g. 'time taken to finish a race' or 'weight of an athlete'.
2) All the fitness tests (see pages 23-24) give quantitative data, as the results are numbers. You can also use surveys to collect quantitative data.
3) Quantitative data can be represented in tables and graphs, and analysed easily.

## Analyse Graphs to spot Trends

Quantitative data is made up of numbers, so you can talk about increases and decreases, and highest and lowest values. This can also help you to spot trends and make predictions.

**A trend is when a graph is generally going up or down over time.**

Here's an example of how data on performance can be analysed as part of feedback (see p47), to help a performer improve.

*Predicting a trend can be tough.*

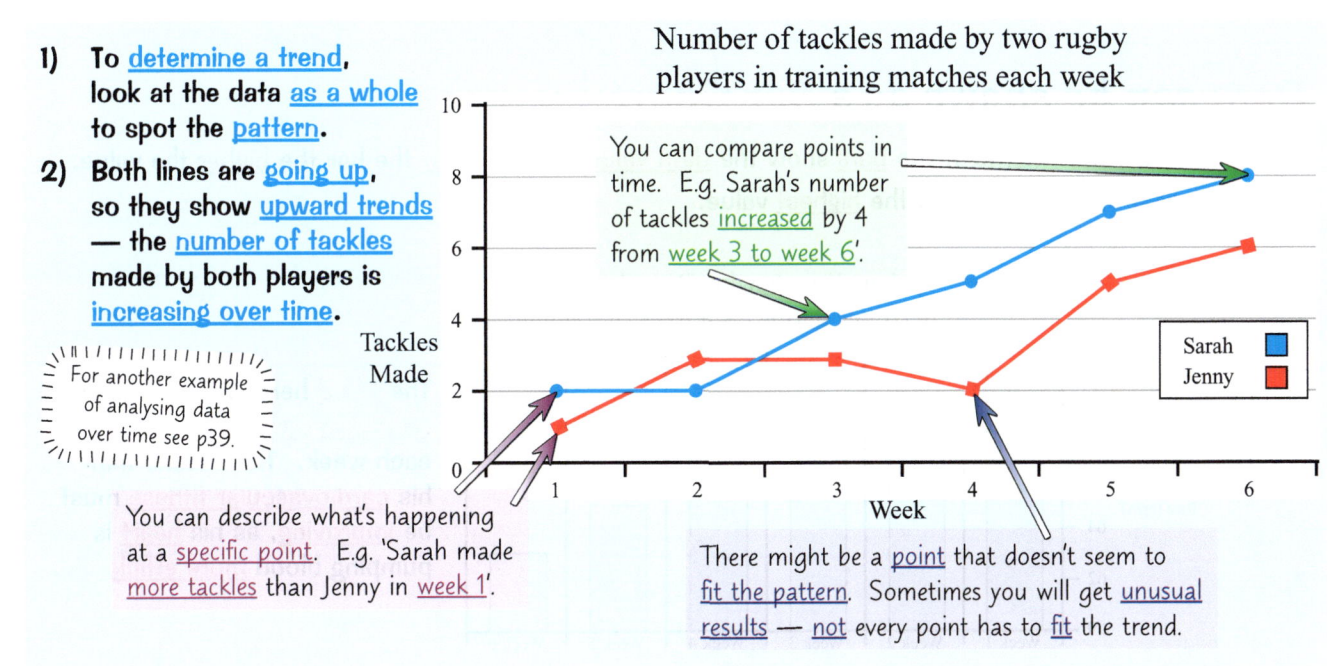

1) To determine a trend, look at the data as a whole to spot the pattern.
2) Both lines are going up, so they show upward trends — the number of tackles made by both players is increasing over time.

*For another example of analysing data over time see p39.*

**Number of tackles made by two rugby players in training matches each week**

You can compare points in time. E.g. 'Sarah's number of tackles increased by 4 from week 3 to week 6'.

You can describe what's happening at a specific point. E.g. 'Sarah made more tackles than Jenny in week 1'.

There might be a point that doesn't seem to fit the pattern. Sometimes you will get unusual results — not every point has to fit the trend.

### Trends about data — amount of boredom is increasing over time...

Just from my experiences writing this page, I can promise you that it's frustratingly easy to mix up the words qualitative and quantitative, so double-check you're using the right one. Exam Practice Question time...

Q1 Using the line graph above, identify which person had the bigger increase in tackles made from week 2 to week 6. [1 mark]

# Using Data

Using data to help you evaluate and plan fitness training is dead important, so here's a whole page on it. You need to understand what the data is showing you as well as use your knowledge about physical fitness.

## You can Analyse your Fitness over Time

1) You can measure the effect of your training by doing regular fitness tests, and comparing the data you get over time.
2) You need to be able to describe what the data shows, and say what this means about the training — i.e. if it's working or what changes are needed.
3) Here's an example of the kind of thing you might see in the exam:

Bryan is doing a training programme to improve his cardiovascular fitness and his muscular endurance...

### Bryan's Fitness Test Results

| Fitness Test | Weeks | | | | | |
|---|---|---|---|---|---|---|
| | 1 | 2 | 3 | 4 | 5 | 6 |
| Cooper 12-minute Run (distance in m) | 1450 | 1490 | 1530 | 1600 | 1640 | 1690 |
| One-Minute Sit-up test (no. of sit-ups) | 45 | 46 | 45 | 46 | 44 | 45 |

The Cooper's Run data shows that Bryan is doing better at the Cooper 12-minute Run Test each week — he is running further in 12 minutes. So the training is improving Bryan's cardiovascular fitness.

The sit-ups data shows that the number of sit-ups Bryan can do is staying about the same, so the training is not improving his abdominal muscular endurance. This means Bryan may want to change his training programme to include more exercises that help improve his abdominal muscular endurance.

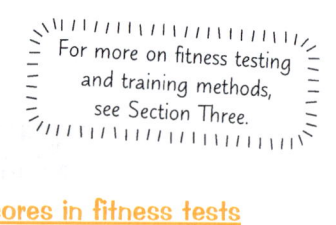

For more on fitness testing and training methods, see Section Three.

You can also look at national averages or ratings tables to understand how your scores in fitness tests compare with others in your age group or gender. For an example of this, see page 24.

## Data can be shown as a Bar Chart

On a bar chart, the heights of the bars show the data values — the taller the bar the higher the value. So, the tallest bar will represent the highest value.

Week 1 has the tallest bar, so Bryan's resting heart rate was highest in week 1.

A bar chart showing Bryan's resting heart rate during each week of training

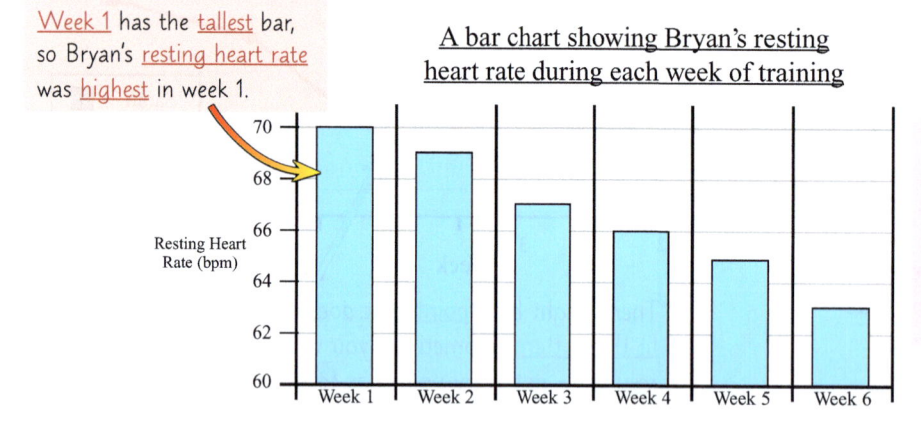

The trend here is that Bryan's resting heart rate is decreasing each week. This means that his cardiovascular fitness must be improving, as his heart is pumping blood more efficiently.

## Top of the charts again — give it up for the 'tallest bars'...

It's really important you get good at using data about fitness to evaluate how effective an exercise programme is. Have another look over pages 23 and 24 to check you know all the fitness tests. Then do this Practice Question...

Q1  Using the bar chart above, what is Bryan's resting heart rate in week 4?

    **A** 70 bpm      **B** 66 bpm      **C** 67 bpm      **D** 100 bpm      [1 mark]

# Using Data

More data?  Well okay, go on then — I know how much you love it.  This page is about delicious pie charts and other less delicious uses of data.  Needless to say, you have to learn it all, tasty or not so tasty...

## You can Look at Data for Large Groups of People

You can also use data to understand what's going on for large groups of people.

*For examples of using data to understand trends on a large scale, see pages 39, 50 and 52.*

1) Pie charts are a good way to compare different categories.
2) The amount of the whole chart a section takes up tells you the percentage in that category — the whole chart represents 100% (everybody).
3) These charts show that the netball club is almost entirely female, the football club is mostly male, and the badminton club is 50% male and 50% female.

Percentage of members of three sports clubs who are male and female

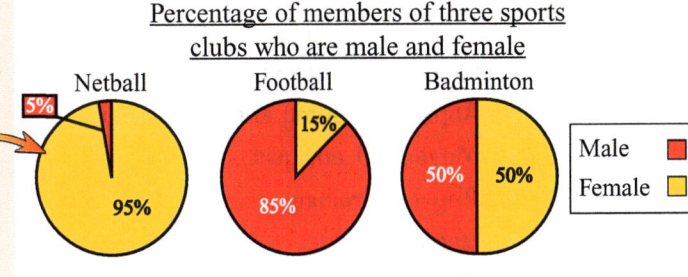

Netball: 5% Male, 95% Female
Football: 15% Male, 85% Female
Badminton: 50% Male, 50% Female

Remember, percentages tell you the proportion of people in a category, not the actual number.

## You can use Data to see the Effects of something

You might be asked to use data to assess the effectiveness of a decision.

### EXAMPLE

1) Organisers of a regional Rugby Union tournament were becoming concerned at the high number of players being sin-binned during the competition.  A player is sent to the 'sin-bin' for repeatedly breaking the rules or for a really bad foul. 
2) From 2012, the organisers introduced a fine for the player being sin-binned to try and discourage players from foul play.
3) The table below shows the number of 'sin-bins' awarded at the tournament each year, from 2007 to 2015.  You can analyse this data to see whether or not the fine has been effective:

Total number of sin-bins awarded each year — The fine is introduced here.

| Year | 2007 | 2008 | 2009 | 2010 | 2011 | 2012 | 2013 | 2014 | 2015 |
|---|---|---|---|---|---|---|---|---|---|
| No. of 'sin-bins' | 8 | 7 | 12 | 13 | 15 | 10 | 8 | 7 | 6 |

4) The fine will have been effective if it has led to fewer sin-bins.
5) As there has been a decrease in sin-bins awarded every year since the introduction of the fine, it looks like the fine has been effective.
6) Plotting a line graph of the data makes it easier to see the patterns.

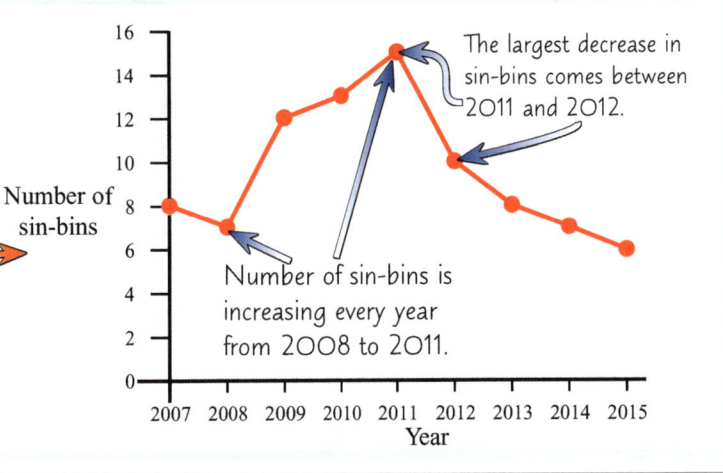

The largest decrease in sin-bins comes between 2011 and 2012.

Number of sin-bins is increasing every year from 2008 to 2011.

## Mmmmmm — pie charts....

That's it, the data section is over.  I know, time flies when you're having fun.  One last Practice Question for you...

Q1  Using the line graph above, state which year had the highest number of sin-bins awarded.  [1 mark]

# Answering Exam Questions

Hurray — you made it to the end of the book. Now there's just the tiny matter (ahem) of the exams left to go. Here's what to expect in your exams and some exam tips to help you on your way to GCSE PE victory.

## You'll Sit Two Exams for PE

1) Each paper will test you on one component of GCSE PE:

### Paper 1 — Component 1

1) Component 1 is called 'Fitness and Body Systems'.
2) It includes the topics:
   - Applied anatomy and physiology
   - Movement analysis
   - Physical training
   - Use of data
3) The first three topics are covered in sections 1-3 of this book (pages 1-35). 'Use of data' is in section 7 (pages 55-57).

### Paper 2 — Component 2

1) Component 2 is called 'Health and Performance'.
2) It includes the topics:
   - Health, fitness and well-being
   - Sport psychology
   - Socio-cultural influences
   - Use of data
3) The first three topics are covered in sections 4-6 of this book (pages 36-54). 'Use of data' is in section 7 (pages 55-57).

2) Paper 1 is worth 90 marks and lasts 1 hour 45 minutes.
3) Paper 2 is worth 70 marks and lasts 1 hour 15 minutes.

## Your Exams are made up of Three Types of Question

### Multiple-Choice — Cross the Right Box

1) The multiple-choice questions give you a choice of four possible answers to the question. All you need to do is cross the box next to the correct answer. They're worth one mark each.
2) Sounds easy enough, but you still need to really know your stuff to be able to get them right.
3) Make sure you only cross one box — if you cross more than one you won't get the mark.
4) Don't worry if you make a mistake and want to change your answer. Just put a horizontal line through the box next to the wrong answer, then cross the box next to your new answer.
5) If you don't know the answer to a question, guess. You don't lose marks for putting a wrong answer — if you guess, you've at least got a chance of getting it right.
6) These questions will be worth a total of eight marks in paper 1 and six marks in paper 2.

### Short-Answer Questions

1) Short-answer questions are usually worth between one and four marks.
2) Make sure you read the question carefully. If you're asked for two influences, make sure you give two, otherwise you won't get the marks.
3) To get the marks, you'll need to show your PE knowledge, apply it to a situation, or use it to analyse or evaluate something. In questions worth more marks, you might need to do a combination of these.
4) These questions will be worth a total of 64 marks in paper 1 and 46 marks in paper 2.

### Extended Writing Questions

1) Extended writing questions are worth a whopping nine marks.
2) To answer these questions, as well as showing and applying your PE knowledge, you'll need to weigh up the advantages and disadvantages of something. Then at the end, you'll need to bring it all together in a conclusion where you make a judgement.
3) These questions will be worth 18 marks in each paper — there will be two per paper.

# Answering Exam Questions

## You get Marks for Meeting Different Assessment Objectives

1) Assessment objectives (AOs) are the things you need to do to get marks in the exams.
2) In each paper, you'll be tested on three AOs:

> Assessment objective 1 (AO1) is all about demonstrating knowledge and understanding of a topic.
> 1) Questions that test AO1 usually ask you to state, define, describe or identify something.
> 2) They could also get you to label a diagram or complete a table or sentence.

> Assessment objective 2 (AO2) is about applying knowledge and understanding of a topic to a context.
> 1) Questions that assess AO2 might ask you to explain why or how something happens.
> 2) You'll sometimes need to give examples to back up your points.

> Assessment objective 3 (AO3) is about analysing and evaluating.
> 1) Questions that test AO3 often start with words like analyse, evaluate, assess, discuss or justify.
> 2) Analysing just means breaking something down into parts or stages to explain it. This can include analysing data to explain what it shows.
> 3) To evaluate, assess or discuss something, you will need to weigh up its advantages and disadvantages in the context given in the question.
> 4) Justifying something means giving reasons why it's sensible.

3) A lot of questions will test more than one assessment objective — for example, if a question tells you to evaluate something (AO3), you'll also need to demonstrate your knowledge of the topic (AO1) and apply it to the situation in the question (AO2).

## In the Exams — Read the Questions and Don't Panic

1) Read every question carefully.
2) The number of marks each question is worth is shown next to it in brackets, or at the bottom of the answer lines. This can be a good guide to the number of points you need to make and how long your answer should be.

    *The number of answer lines given in a question can also be a good guide to how much to write.*

3) Make sure your answers are clear and easy to read. If the examiner can't read your handwriting, they won't be able to give you any marks.
4) Don't panic — if you get stuck on a question, just move on to the next one. You can come back to it if you have time at the end.

## Have a look at this Example Question and Answer

1) This example exam answer will show you how marks are awarded for the things you write:

> 15  Figure 1 shows a performer taking part in archery.
>     Assess the importance of agility to the archer.
>
> **Figure 1**
>
> AO1 → Agility is the ability to change body position or direction quickly and with control.
> AO2 → Archers need to keep their body in a still, steady position so that they can aim accurately at the target.
>        Therefore, agility is not an important component of fitness for an archer. ← AO3
>
> Total for Question 15 = 3 marks

2) This answer gets one mark for each assessment objective it meets.
3) It meets AO1 by defining agility, AO2 by explaining what impact agility has on an archer, and AO3 by evaluating the importance of agility for the archer.

Answering Exam Questions

# Answers

**A note about answers and marks**
The answers and mark schemes given here should be used mainly for guidance, as there may be many different correct answers to each question — don't panic if your answers are a bit different.

## Section One — Anatomy and Physiology

### Page 1 — The Skeletal System
**Q1** E.g. The main function of long bones is to allow movement *[1 mark]*. This function makes participation in physical activity and sport possible because it allows a performer to carry out specific sporting movements *[1 mark]*.

### Page 2 — The Skeletal System
**Q1** C Metacarpal *[1 mark]*

### Page 4 — The Muscular System
**Q1** The hip flexors *[1 mark]*
When kicking a football, the hip flexors allow flexion at the hip so the entire leg swings forward.

### Page 5 — The Muscular System
**Q1** A Type I *[1 mark]*
Type I muscle fibres are better suited to long periods of exercise than other muscle fibre types.

### Page 6 — The Cardiovascular System
**Q1** E.g. The pulmonary artery carries deoxygenated blood *[1 mark]* to the lungs, where it becomes oxygenated *[1 mark]*. This is essential for physical activity and sport as this oxygenated blood can then be delivered to the muscles *[1 mark]* to provide the oxygen needed for exercise *[1 mark]*.

### Page 7 — The Cardiovascular System
**Q1** E.g. Plasma carries everything in the bloodstream *[1 mark]*. Firstly, it carries red blood cells, which are needed to deliver oxygen that muscles need during exercise *[1 mark]*. Secondly, it carries digested food in the form of glucose. This glucose is needed for respiration to release the energy needed for physical activity *[1 mark]*. Finally, plasma takes away the waste products that muscles produce during exercise *[1 mark]*.

### Page 8 — The Respiratory System
**Q1** E.g. Deoxygenated blood becomes oxygenated through gas exchange between the capillaries containing the deoxygenated blood and the alveoli containing oxygen *[1 mark]*. Oxygen diffuses from an area of higher concentration (the alveoli) *[1 mark]* to an area of lower concentration (the deoxygenated blood) *[1 mark]*.

### Page 9 — The Respiratory System
**Q1** E.g. An athlete with a high vital capacity can breathe in a large amount of oxygen and can breathe out a large amount of carbon dioxide *[1 mark]*. This is beneficial to an athlete because it means that more oxygen can be delivered to the muscles to allow them to move during physical activity *[1 mark]*. It also means that more carbon dioxide can be carried away from the muscles and out of the body *[1 mark]*.

### Page 10 — Aerobic and Anaerobic Exercise
**Q1** E.g. A 100 metre sprint would be an anaerobic activity because it is a high intensity and short duration event *[1 mark]*. In the time taken to run 100 metres, the body systems would be unable to deliver oxygen quickly enough for the muscles to use aerobic respiration *[1 mark]*, so the muscles would release energy without oxygen *[1 mark]*.

### Page 11 — Short-Term Effects of Exercise
**Q1** During exercise, the **heart rate** *[1 mark]* and stroke volume increase. This leads to an increase in the **cardiac** *[1 mark]* output so more oxygenated **blood** *[1 mark]* is delivered to the muscles.

**Q2** E.g. A footballer experiencing muscle fatigue may be unable to sprint with the ball. This could make them less likely to score a goal *[1 mark]*.

### Page 12 — Short-Term Effects of Exercise
**Q1** a) 63 cm³ *[1 mark]*
b) 141 cm³ *[1 mark]*
Stroke volume increases during exercise and slowly returns to normal after exercise has stopped. So the lowest value in the table must have been recorded before exercise started, and the highest must have been during exercise.

### Page 13 — Long-Term Effects of Exercise
**Q1** E.g. Muscle hypertrophy means an increase in muscle thickness *[1 mark]*. This would benefit a performer participating in weightlifting because it would increase their strength *[1 mark]*, meaning they would be able to lift heavier weights *[1 mark]*.

## Section Two — Movement Analysis

### Page 15 — Lever Systems
**Q1** Third class *[1 mark]*
During flexion of the knee, the lever arm is the lower leg (below the knee), the fulcrum is the knee joint and the load is the weight of the lower leg and the foot. The effort is the force of the hamstrings pulling the lever arm below the knee.

### Page 16 — Planes and Axes of Movement
**Q1** Frontal plane *[1 mark]* and sagittal axis *[1 mark]*
A star jump involves abduction and adduction of the arms and legs. These movements use the frontal plane and sagittal axis.

# Answers

## Section Three — Physical Training

### Page 18 — Health and Fitness

**Q1** E.g. An athlete could train too much *[1 mark]*. This might give them a high level of fitness, but cause them to get injured *[1 mark]*.

### Page 19 — Components of Fitness

**Q1** E.g. Muscular endurance allows you to repeatedly use voluntary muscles without getting tired *[1 mark]*. A long-distance cyclist uses the same leg muscles over a long period of time *[1 mark]*, so muscular endurance is very important in preventing fatigue in the later stages of a race and in helping the cyclist to sprint at the end *[1 mark]*.

*Any reasonable application of muscular endurance to a cycling race will get you the third mark here.*

### Page 20 — Components of Fitness

**Q1** E.g. Flexibility will help the swimmer avoid injury, meaning they can train more, which will help them perform better *[1 mark]*. Flexibility will help the swimmer achieve longer/more efficient strokes *[1 mark]*.

### Page 21 — Components of Fitness

**Q1** E.g. Coordination is the ability to use two or more parts of the body together, efficiently and accurately *[1 mark]*.

*Make sure your definition talks about using two or more parts of the body, and you'll get the mark.*

E.g. A boxer needs good hand-eye coordination to be able to throw a punch accurately *[1 mark]*.

*Any example of using two or more body parts together in boxing is okay for the second mark.*

### Page 22 — Components of Fitness

**Q1** E.g. A rugby player uses power to kick the ball a long way *[1 mark]* and to tackle another player to the ground *[1 mark]*.

*Remember that power is a combination of strength and speed. There are lots of other examples — e.g. jumping for the ball or sprinting for the try line.*

### Page 23 — Fitness Testing

**Q1** Strength (or 'muscular strength') *[1 mark]*

### Page 24 — Fitness Testing

**Q1** C Average *[1 mark]*

*Sarah's female and her time of 5.7 s falls between 5.60 s and 5.89 s — it's in the 'Average' column.*

### Page 25 — Principles of Training

**Q1** E.g. A rower could train using a rowing machine *[1 mark]*, as this would work the same muscles as they use in their sport *[1 mark]*.

### Page 26 — Principles of Training

**Q1** E.g. Overtraining means not allowing enough time between training sessions for your body to recover *[1 mark]*. It can lead to injury, which will stop you training and lead to a decrease in fitness *[1 mark]*.

### Page 27 — Training Target Zones

**Q1** 220 − 35 = 185 *[1 mark]*
185 × 0.8 *[1 mark]* = 148 bpm *[1 mark]*

*The first mark is for finding the maximum heart rate (220 − age). The second mark is for using the right decimal for the threshold. And the last mark is for getting the maths right and getting the correct answer.*

### Page 28 — Training Methods

**Q1** E.g. Continuous training is good aerobic training *[1 mark]*. This means it is well suited to aerobic endurance activities like marathon running *[1 mark]*. However, continuous training does not improve anaerobic fitness *[1 mark]*, so is not well suited to anaerobic activities like sprinting *[1 mark]*.

### Page 29 — Training Methods

**Q1** E.g. For strength training, an athlete needs to use a high weight and do a low number of reps *[1 mark]*. They can overload by gradually increasing the weight used *[1 mark]*.

### Page 30 — Training Methods

**Q1** E.g. Plyometric training increases power *[1 mark]*, which would help the basketball player to jump higher *[1 mark]*, increasing their ability to make interceptions *[1 mark]*.

*One mark is for saying plyometric training improves power. One mark is for identifying an action that power helps with — e.g. jumping, sprinting, shooting. And one mark is for linking this to a specific basketball skill — e.g. lay-ups are easier when you can jump higher / sprinting faster allows you to get past opponents / a more powerful shot will help you to score three-point shots.*

### Page 31 — Preventing Injuries

**Q1** *This mark scheme gives examples of some points you might have made in your answer, and how many marks you'd get for making those points. You can still get full marks if you haven't written every individual point below, as long as the points you've made are detailed enough.*

*You will get up to three marks for showing knowledge and understanding of a warm-up, for example:*

- A warm-up includes light aerobic exercise to gradually increase your pulse rate.
- A warm-up includes stretching the muscles that will be used in the activity.
- A warm-up can include practice actions to prepare the muscles that will be used during the activity.

*You will get up to six marks if you also include examples of how the warm-up can help prevent injuries in hockey, for example:*

- Practising passing the ball in the warm-up helps prepare the shoulder and arm muscles for passing during the hockey match, so they're warm and less likely to get injured.
- Stretching the leg muscles will help to improve their flexibility, which will help the player to avoid injury when they lunge to reach the ball.
- The light exercise eases the player's body into more intense exercise, which helps them to avoid injury when they need to sprint to outrun other players during the hockey match.

*You will get up to nine marks if you also evaluate the importance of a warm-up in preventing injury. You can include comparisons with other methods of preventing injury in a hockey match. For example:*

# Answers

- A warm-up is necessary for a hockey player to avoid injury, because stretching and practice actions help prepare the player's muscles for the strenuous actions they'll perform in the match, like lunging for the ball or sprinting.
- However, it is also important to play by the rules to avoid injury, as foul play using a hockey stick can lead to serious injuries. Protective equipment, such as gumshields and shinpads, is also necessary to prevent injuries.
- In conclusion, a warm-up is absolutely vital before a hockey match to help prevent injury. However a warm-up alone is not sufficient to prevent all types of injury, so other measures must also be taken.

*[9 marks available in total]*

## Page 32 — Injuries and Treatment

**Q1** Ligaments (or 'a ligament') *[1 mark]*

Sprains are joint injuries where the ligament has been stretched or torn.

## Page 33 — Injuries and Treatment

**Q1** You can use the RICE method to treat a sprain *[1 mark]*. The injured person should stop and rest, apply ice and a bandage to their ankle and elevate it above their heart *[1 mark]*.

It's not enough to just write RICE here — make sure you apply it to the specific injury to get 2 marks.

## Page 34 — Performance-Enhancing Drugs

**Q1** E.g. An archer might use beta blockers because beta blockers have a calming effect and steady shaking hands *[1 mark]*, which will help the archer keep steady as they take aim and shoot *[1 mark]*.

There are a few different performance-enhancing drugs that an archer could use to help them compete. The first mark comes from explaining what the drug does. And the second mark comes from applying that effect to archery.

# Section Four — Health, Fitness and Well-being

## Page 36 — Health, Fitness and Well-being

**Q1** Either:
You are far more at risk of type-2 diabetes when you are overweight *[1 mark]*. Exercise helps you to maintain a healthy weight, so helps prevent type-2 diabetes. *[1 mark]*.
Or:
Exercise helps to improve your insulin sensitivity *[1 mark]*. This means you are less likely to become insulin-resistant, so are less likely to get type-2 diabetes. *[1 mark]*.

## Page 37 — Health, Fitness and Well-being

**Q1** Any two from: e.g.
Exercise relieves stress/tension / it can help you learn to cope with pressure/manage emotions / it can increase self-esteem and confidence / it can increase your levels of endorphins, which makes you feel good *[1 mark for each]*.

You need to give two benefits for two marks — so you don't need to go into any depth.

## Page 38 — Lifestyle Choices

**Q1** E.g. Chemicals in the smoke damage cilia *[1 mark]*. This increases the risk of infection of the airways *[1 mark]*, which can lead to bronchitis *[1 mark]*.

There are lots of different answers you can give here — just make sure that you say enough to get three marks. You get one mark for naming the health problem, one for explaining the damage that smoking causes and one for saying how that damage causes the disease.

## Page 39 — Sedentary Lifestyle

**Q1** Any two from: e.g.
Osteoporosis / depression / high blood pressure / coronary heart disease / diabetes *[1 mark for each]*.

## Page 40 — Diet and Nutrition

**Q1** Carbohydrates *[1 mark]*

Remember that macronutrients are carbohydrates, proteins and fats.

## Page 41 — Diet and Nutrition

**Q1** E.g. Exercise causes your body temperature to rise *[1 mark]*. This means you lose water through sweating as your body tries to keep cool, which could cause dehydration *[1 mark]*.

You also lose water through breathing. Exercise makes you breathe more frequently and heavily, so this could also dehydrate you.

## Page 42 — Diet, Nutrition and Performance

**Q1** The triathlete would benefit more from carbohydrate loading *[1 mark]*. This is because the triathlon is an endurance event, so the triathlete's muscles will need a large amount of stored energy to last a long time *[1 mark]*. Weightlifting is a short duration event, so the weightlifter doesn't need as much stored energy *[1 mark]*.

## Page 43 — Optimum Weight

**Q1** Any two from: e.g.
They could have different bone structures / different muscle girths / compete in different types of events that have different weight requirements *[1 mark for each]*.

# Section Five — Sport Psychology

## Page 45 — Skills and Practice

**Q1** E.g. Distributed practice may be useful for improving a dismount in gymnastics because it includes breaks between practice *[1 mark]*. A dismount is a complex skill that requires high levels of concentration to perform *[1 mark]*, so it might help the gymnast to rest between practice intervals in order to prevent mental and physical fatigue which could lead to injury *[1 mark]*.

You could also say that taking breaks during practice would allow the gymnast to mentally rehearse the dismount, or to receive feedback on how well they performed it.

# Answers

## Page 46 — Goal Setting

**Q1** E.g. This goal does not apply the 'measurable' principle *[1 mark]*. It is not measurable because it does not say how much faster the athlete would like to run *[1 mark]*.

You could also say that the goal doesn't apply the 'specific' principle for the same reason.

## Page 47 — Guidance and Feedback

**Q1** This mark scheme gives examples of some points you might have made in your answer, and how many marks you'd get for making those points. You can still get full marks if you haven't written every individual point below, as long as the points you've made are detailed enough.

You will get up to three marks for showing knowledge and understanding of the different types of guidance, for example:

- Verbal guidance includes instructions given in words.
- Verbal guidance involves a coach explaining how to perform a skill.
- Manual guidance involves a coach moving the performer's body through a technique.

You will get up to six marks if you also apply your knowledge of guidance to a beginner in golf, for example:

- Verbal guidance could include the coach telling the learner how to position their legs before swinging the club.
- Manual guidance could include the coach moving the learner's arms through a golf swing.
- Verbal and manual guidance could be used at the same time. For example, the coach could manually position the learner's hands on the club, while explaining how they should be positioned.

You will get up to nine marks if you also evaluate which guidance type would be best for use with a beginner golfer. For example:

- Manual guidance can be useful for beginners as it gives them the feel of the correct technique. However, it can lead to the learner relying on it.
- Verbal guidance alone may be confusing for a beginner, as they may be unable to picture how a technique should feel due to their limited experience in golf.
- In conclusion, it would be best to combine verbal and manual guidance to improve a beginner's performance in golf. This would allow the learner to experience how golfing techniques feel while having them explained by the coach, to make sure they understand them.

*[9 marks available in total]*

# Section Six — Sport, Society and Culture

## Page 49 — Influences on Participation

**Q1** Any two from: e.g. You might not be able to afford to play the sports you want to / you might live in an area that doesn't have sports facilities / you might not have access to transport to facilities / you might work irregular hours that mean you can't join local teams *[1 mark for each]*.

You could write an answer to this question the other way round — e.g. if you have plenty of money you can afford to play many different sports.

## Page 50 — Influences on Participation

**Q1** B Cycling *[1 mark]*

## Page 51 — Commercialisation of Sport

**Q1** E.g. Media coverage of sports creates role models *[1 mark]*. This can inspire people watching the sport to participate *[1 mark]*. Media coverage of a sport allows it to reach a much larger audience *[1 mark]*. This means that more people will become aware of the sport and learn about it, which may encourage them to take it up *[1 mark]*.

With each point, make sure you say enough to get two marks by saying how the media's coverage of sport encourages people to take part.

## Page 52 — Commercialisation of Sport

**Q1** E.g. Sponsorship by a fast-food company would have a positive impact because it would give the team more money *[1 mark]*. This would allow them to buy more equipment or improve facilities *[1 mark]*, helping the team to improve their performance *[1 mark]*. However, by being promoted by the football team, the fast-food company could gain a false image of health *[1 mark]*. As it is an under-12's team, the young players and supporters may be influenced to eat more fast food *[1 mark]*, which could lead to an increased risk of obesity *[1 mark]*.

You get three marks for your 'positive' answer and three marks for your 'negative' answer. To get all three marks in each case you need to explain what effect the sponsorship will have, and why that is good or bad.

## Page 53 — Sporting Behaviour

**Q1** E.g. Deviance is where a participant in a sport breaks the laws of the game *[1 mark]*, whereas gamesmanship only involves bending the rules, without actually breaking them *[1 mark]*.

# Section Seven — Using Data

## Page 55 — Using Data

**Q1** Sarah *[1 mark]*

Sarah had an increase of 6, from 2 tackles to 8. Jenny only increased by 3, from 3 tackles to 6.

## Page 56 — Using Data

**Q1** B 66 bpm *[1 mark]*

## Page 57 — Using Data

**Q1** 2011 *[1 mark]*

# Glossary

| | |
|---|---|
| abduction | Movement away from an imaginary centre line through the body. |
| adduction | Movement towards an imaginary centre line through the body. |
| aerobic respiration | When the body releases energy using glucose and oxygen. Carbon dioxide and water are produced as by-products (waste). |
| agility | The ability to change body position or direction quickly and with control. |
| alveoli | Small air bags in the lungs where gases are exchanged. |
| anaerobic respiration | When the body doesn't have enough oxygen to release energy aerobically, so it just uses glucose. Lactic acid is produced as a by-product (waste). |
| antagonistic muscle pair | A pair of muscles that work together to bring about movement. As one muscle contracts (the agonist) the other relaxes (the antagonist). |
| axis of movement | An imaginary line that the body or a body part can move around. There are three axes you need to know: sagittal, frontal and vertical. |
| balance | The ability to keep the body's centre of mass over a base of support. |
| balanced diet | The best ratio of nutrients to match your lifestyle. |
| basic skill | A simple skill which doesn't need much concentration to do, e.g. running. |
| blood cell | A component of blood. There are red blood cells (which carry oxygen) and white blood cells (which fight disease). |
| blood pressure | How strongly the blood presses against the walls of blood vessels. |
| blood vessel | Part of the cardiovascular system that transports blood around the body. The three main types are arteries, veins and capillaries. |
| body composition | The percentage of body weight made up by fat, muscle and bone. |
| cardiac output | The volume of blood pumped by each ventricle in the heart per minute. |
| cardio-respiratory system | The combination of the cardiovascular and respiratory systems working together to get oxygen into the body tissues and carbon dioxide out of them. |
| cardiovascular fitness (aerobic endurance) | The ability of the heart and lungs to supply oxygen to the muscles, so that the whole body can be exercised for a long time. |
| cardiovascular system | The organs responsible for circulating blood around the body. |
| circumduction | Movement of a limb, hand or foot in a circular motion. |
| closed skill | A skill performed in a predictable environment — it's not affected by external factors. |
| commercialisation | The commercialisation of sport means the transformation of sport into something people can make money from, e.g. through sponsorship. |
| complex skill | A skill which needs lots of concentration to do, e.g. a volley in football. |
| connective tissue | Body tissue that holds other body tissues (e.g. muscles and bones) together. Cartilage, ligaments and tendons are types of connective tissue. |
| cool-down | Light exercise and stretching done after exercise to return your body to normal. |
| coordination | The ability to use two or more parts of the body together, efficiently and accurately. |
| coronary heart disease | When fatty deposits build up in the arteries around the heart, which restrict the flow of blood. |

Glossary

# Glossary

| | |
|---|---|
| data | Information — in words or numbers. Data can be quantitative (numbers) or qualitative (words). |
| deoxygenated blood | Blood that contains low levels of oxygen and high levels of carbon dioxide. |
| deviance | Behaviour that goes against the moral values or laws of the sport. |
| diffusion | The process of substances (e.g. oxygen) moving from a place where there is a higher concentration to a place where there is a lower concentration. |
| dorsi-flexion | Flexion at the ankle by lifting the toes. |
| exercise | A form of physical activity done to maintain or improve health and/or fitness. |
| extension | Opening a joint, e.g. straightening the leg at the knee. |
| feedback | Information received about a performance either during it (concurrent feedback) or after it (terminal feedback). It can be intrinsic (from yourself) or extrinsic (from other sources). |
| fitness | The ability to meet the demands of the environment. |
| flexibility | The amount of movement possible at a joint. |
| flexion | Closing a joint, e.g. bending the arm at the elbow. |
| gamesmanship | Gaining an advantage by using tactics that seem unfair, but aren't against the rules. |
| guidance | Information or help in learning a skill. Guidance can be visual, verbal, manual or mechanical. |
| health | A state of complete physical, mental and social well-being and not merely the absence of disease or infirmity. |
| heart rate | The number of times your heart beats in one minute. It is measured in beats per minute (bpm). |
| high organisation skill | A skill which can't easily be broken down into different parts that can be practised separately, because the parts of the skill are closely linked. E.g. a cartwheel. |
| joint type | The main types of joint are ball and socket, hinge, condyloid and pivot. Each type allows a different range of movement. |
| lactic acid | A waste product produced during anaerobic respiration, making the muscles feel tired (fatigued). |
| lever system | A system that allows the body's muscles to move the bones in the skeleton. A lever system can be first, second or third class, and is made up of a lever arm, effort, fulcrum and load. |
| low organisation skill | A skill which can easily be broken down into different parts that can be practised separately. E.g. the front crawl stroke in swimming. |
| mechanical advantage | When a lever can move a large load with a small amount of effort from the muscles. |
| mechanical disadvantage | When a lever requires a large effort from the muscles to move a small load. |
| the media | Organisations involved in mass communication — e.g. through television, radio, newspapers and the Internet. |
| muscle fibre | One of the fibres that make up the muscles in the body. There are three main types: type I, type IIA and type IIX. Each type is suited to a different intensity of exercise. |
| muscular endurance | The ability to repeatedly use the voluntary muscles for a long time, without getting tired. |
| musculo-skeletal system | The combination of the muscular and skeletal systems working together to allow movement. |
| obesity | Having a lot more body fat than you should. |

# Glossary

| | |
|---|---|
| open skill | A skill performed in a changing environment, where a performer has to react and adapt to external factors. |
| optimum weight | Roughly what you should weigh for good health, based on your gender, height, bone structure and muscle girth. It can also be affected by the kind of activity or sport you do. |
| overload | Working your body harder to increase fitness levels over time. |
| oxygenated blood | Blood that contains high levels of oxygen and low levels of carbon dioxide. |
| PEP | Personal Exercise Programme. A training programme that's designed to suit a specific person and improve their health, fitness or performance. |
| performance | How well a task is completed. |
| plane of movement | An imaginary flat surface used to describe the direction of a movement. The body or a body part moves in a plane. There are three planes you need to know: sagittal, transverse and frontal. |
| plantar-flexion | Extension at the ankle by pointing the toes. |
| power | A combination of speed and strength. |
| practice | When a skill is repeated to improve it. The types of practice are massed, distributed, fixed and variable. |
| reaction time | The time taken to move in response to a stimulus. |
| respiratory system | The organs in the body used for breathing. |
| rotation | Movement of the body or a body part in a clockwise or anticlockwise motion. |
| sedentary lifestyle | A lifestyle where there is little, irregular or no physical activity. |
| SMART | The five principles of goal setting — it stands for Specific, Measurable, Achievable, Realistic and Time-bound. |
| socio-economic group | A way of grouping people based on their job, how much money they have and where they live, e.g. 'working class' is a socio-economic group. |
| speed | The rate at which someone is able to move, or to cover a distance in a given amount of time. |
| sponsorship | When a company pays to associate their name with some part of a sport, including individual sportspeople. It's usually done to make money. |
| sportsmanship | Being honest, sticking to the rules and treating your opponents with respect. |
| strength | The amount of force that a muscle or muscle group can apply against a resistance. |
| stroke volume | The volume of blood pumped with each heartbeat by each ventricle in the heart. |
| tidal volume | The amount of air that is breathed in or out in one breath. |
| trend | When a graph is generally going up or down over time. |
| vertebral column | The bones (vertebrae) making up the spine/spinal column. The vertebral column has five regions: cervical, thoracic, lumbar, the sacrum and the coccyx. |
| vital capacity | The most air you can possibly breathe in after breathing out the largest volume of air possible. |
| warm-up | Preparing your body for exercise. It's made up of three main phases: light exercise, stretching and practice actions. |

# Index

30 m sprint test 23

## A
abduction 3, 4, 16
abrasions 32
adaptations 26
adduction 3, 4, 16
advertising 51, 52
aerobic
  exercise 10, 27
  respiration 10
  target zones 27
  training 28-30
aerobic endurance 19
aerobics 30
agility 21, 23
agonists 5
air 9
alcohol 38
alveoli 8, 13, 38
amino acids 40
anabolic steroids 34
anaerobic
  exercise 10, 27
  respiration 10
  target zones 27
  training 28-30
antagonistic muscle pairs 5
antagonists 5
aorta 6
arteries 7, 13, 36, 38
arterioles 7
atrium 6
average ratings (fitness tests) 24
axes (of movement) 16

## B
balance 21, 30
balanced diet 40
ball and socket joints 3
bar charts 56
beta blockers 34
biceps 4, 5, 15, 29
blood 6, 7
  pressure 13, 36, 38, 39
  vessels 7
blood doping 34, 53
body composition 20, 28
body fat 39, 42, 43
BODYPUMP™ 30
bone density 13
bones 1, 2
  injuries 33
bone structure 43
breathing 8, 9
breathing rate 11
bronchi 8
bronchioles 8

## C
capillaries 7, 8, 13
carbohydrate loading 42
carbohydrates 10, 40, 42
carbon dioxide 8, 9, 12
cardiac muscle 4
cardiac output 11-13
cardio-respiratory system
    8, 12, 13, 36
cardiovascular fitness
    13, 19, 23, 28-30
cardiovascular system 6, 7, 11, 12
cartilage 3, 32
centre of mass 21
cilia 38
circuit training 29
circumduction 3, 4
commercialisation 51, 52
components of fitness 19-22
concentration gradient 8, 12
concussion 33
condyloid joints 3
connective tissues 3
continuous training 28
cool-down 31
Cooper 12-minute run/swim test 23
coordination 21

## D
data 12, 24, 39, 50, 52, 55-57
  tables 24, 56, 57
dehydration 41
deltoids 4
deoxygenated blood 6, 8
deviance 53
diabetes 36
diaphragm 8, 13
diet 38, 40-42
diffusion 8, 12
disabilities 50
dislocation 32
diuretics 34
dorsi-flexion 3, 4
dynamometer 23

## E
effort 15
emotional benefits of exercise 37
energy 10
energy balance 43
EPO 34
exercise 18
  benefits of 36, 37
  long-term effects 13
  short-term effects 11, 12
extension 3, 4, 16
external intercostals 8, 13
external obliques 4

## F
fartlek training 28
fats 10, 40, 42
feedback 47, 55
fibre 41
fibres (muscles) 5
fitness 18, 36
  components of 19-22
  data 24, 56
  testing 23, 24
fitness classes 30
FITT 26
flat bones 1, 2
flexibility 20, 24, 30
flexion 3, 4, 15, 16
fractures 33
fulcrum 15

## G
gamesmanship 53
gastrocnemius 4, 5
gender divide 49
glucose 10
gluteus maximus 4, 5
goal setting 46
golfer's elbow 32
graphs 12, 39, 50, 52, 55-57
grip dynamometer test 23
growth hormones 34
guidance 47

## H
hamstrings 4, 5
hand-eye coordination 21
Harvard step test 23
health 18, 36, 37
  emotional 37
  physical 36
  social 37
heart 6, 13
heart disease 36, 38
heart rate 11-13, 27
hinge joints 3
hip flexors 4, 5
hypertrophy 13

## I
Illinois agility run test 23
individual needs 25
injuries 26, 32, 33
  preventing 20, 31
insulin 36
intensities of exercise 26, 27
interval training 28
involuntary muscles 4, 19
irregular bones 1, 2

# Index

**J**
joints 3, 5
  injuries 32

**L**
lactate accumulation 11
lactic acid 9-11
latissimus dorsi 4
levers 15
lifestyle choices 38
ligaments 3, 13, 32
load 15
long bones 1, 2
lungs 8, 13, 38
  capacity 13

**M**
maximum heart rate 27
mechanical advantage 15
mechanical disadvantage 15
media 51
mental preparation 31, 45
mental rehearsal 45
minerals 1, 41
muscle fibres 5
muscle girth 13, 43
muscles 4
  antagonistic pairs 5
  attachment 1, 2
  fatigue 11
  hypertrophy 13
  injuries 32
  repairing 40, 42
muscular endurance 13, 19, 23, 28-30
muscular system 4, 5, 11
musculo-skeletal system 4, 13, 36

**N**
narcotic analgesics 34
nutrients 40

**O**
obesity 36, 39
one-minute press-up/sit-up test 23
optimum weight 43
osteoporosis 36
overfat 39
overload 25, 26
overtraining 26
overweight 39
oxygen 8, 9, 12
oxygenated blood 6, 8
oxygen debt 11, 12

**P**
Paralympics 50
PARQ 31
participation rates 49, 50
pectoralis major 4
peptide hormones 34
performance 18
performance-enhancing drugs 34, 53
personal exercise programme (PEP) 25, 26, 38
physical benefits of exercise 36
pie charts 57
Pilates 30
pivot joints 3
planes (of movement) 16
plantar-flexion 3, 4
plasma 7
platelets 1, 7
plyometric training 30
posture 20, 39
power 22, 24, 30
practice 45
principles of training 25, 26, 31
progressive overload 25
proteins 40, 42
pulled hamstring 32
pulmonary artery 6
pulmonary veins 6

**Q**
quadriceps 4, 5, 30
qualitative data 55
quantitative data 55

**R**
racism 49
reaction time 22
recovery 26
recovery position 33
recreational drugs 38
red blood cells 1, 7, 13
rehydration 41
reps 29
resistance training 29
respiration 10
respiratory system 8, 9, 11, 12
resting heart rate 11, 13
reversibility 26
RICE 33
role models 51
rotation 3, 4, 16

**S**
sedentary lifestyle 39
serotonin 37
short bones 1, 2
sit and reach test 24
skeletal system 1-3
skills 45
skin injuries 32
sleep 38
SMART 46
smoking 38
social benefits of exercise 37
socio-economic groups 49
soft-tissue injuries 32
specificity 25
speed 20, 23, 28
spine 2
Spinning® 30
sponsorship 51, 52
sports drinks 41
sportsmanship 53
sprains 32, 33
sprint tests 23
stimulants 34
strains 32, 33
strength 13, 19, 23, 29, 30
stress 37
strokes 36, 38
stroke volume 11-13
sweating 7, 41

**T**
tendons 3, 13, 32
tennis elbow 32
testosterone 34
tibialis anterior 4, 5
tidal volume 9
time-wasting 53
trachea 8
training methods 28-30
training target zones 27
trends 39, 52, 55
triceps 4, 5
type-2 diabetes 36

**V**
valves (heart) 6
vascular shunting 7
vasoconstriction 7
vasodilation 7
veins 7, 13
vena cava 6
ventricles 6
venules 7
vertical jump test 24
vital capacity 9, 13
vitamins 41
voluntary muscles 4, 19

**W**
warm-up 31, 45
water 41
weight training 29
well-being 18
  emotional 37
  physical 36
  social 37
white blood cells 1, 7
work/rest/sleep balance 38

**Y**
yoga 30